Cambridge Elements ☰

Elements in Publishing and Book Culture
edited by
Samantha Rayner
University College London
Leah Tether
University of Bristol

THE EDITED COLLECTION

Pasts, Present and Futures

Peter Webster
Webster Research and Consulting

CAMBRIDGE
UNIVERSITY PRESS

CAMBRIDGE
UNIVERSITY PRESS

University Printing House, Cambridge CB2 8BS, United Kingdom

One Liberty Plaza, 20th Floor, New York, NY 10006, USA

477 Williamstown Road, Port Melbourne, VIC 3207, Australia

314–321, 3rd Floor, Plot 3, Splendor Forum, Jasola District Centre, New Delhi – 110025, India

79 Anson Road, #06–04/06, Singapore 079906

Cambridge University Press is part of the University of Cambridge.

It furthers the University's mission by disseminating knowledge in the pursuit of education, learning, and research at the highest international levels of excellence.

www.cambridge.org
Information on this title: www.cambridge.org/9781108739375
DOI: 10.1017/9781108683647

First published 2020

A catalogue record for this publication is available from the British Library.

ISBN 978-1-108-73937-5 Paperback
ISSN 2514-8524 (online)
ISSN 2514-8516 (print)

The Edited Collection

Pasts, Present and Futures

Elements in Publishing and Book Culture

DOI: 10.1017/9781108683647

First published online: April 2020

Peter Webster

Webster Research and Consulting

Author for correspondence: Peter Webster, peter@websterresearchconsulting.com

ABSTRACT: Edited collections are widely supposed to contain lesser work than scholarly journals; to be incoherent as volumes, no more than the sum of their parts; and to be less visible to potential readers once published. It is also often taken as axiomatic that those who make decisions in relation to hiring, promotion, tenure and funding agree. To publish in or edit an essay collection is thought to risk being penalised for the format before even a word is read. After examining the origins of this critique, this book explores the modern history of the edited collection and the particular roles it has played. It then examines each component part of the critique, showing that they are either largely unfounded or susceptible of solution. It proposes the edited collection as a model of one possible idea of scholarly community: one of collaboration, trust and mutual obligation in pursuit of a wider good.

KEYWORDS: academic libraries; academic publishing; publishing history

ISBNs: 9781108739375 (PB), 9781108683647 (OC)

ISSNs: 2514-8524 (online), 2514-8516 (print)

Contents

1 Introduction

Robin is a historian in a British university (although he does not in fact exist). He has a short-term teaching contract with the department in which he recently completed his PhD; he has published one of its chapters in a journal which (if his peers are to be believed) seems to be respectably middle-ranking. On his better days Robin very much intends to turn the thesis into his first book, although somehow it seems to be the wrong shape to be easily adapted, and so work on it has so far been slow and without enthusiasm.

Robin has a good friend from another university, called Lucy. Her research is on a similar area, and the two have met regularly at conferences, anxiously trading stories about the academic job market in the faded bars of university halls of residence. They are organising a conference together, at which several mutual friends will deliver papers. They have been in touch with a publisher who (after some delay and many emails) has agreed to consider publishing an edited collection of those papers. It has the working title *Religion, Politics and Culture in Early Modern Europe*.

The conference takes place. In the final session they outline the idea of the book and invite the speakers to submit abstracts of their papers for consideration. A short document of two or three paragraphs is distributed, outlining the theme. After a couple of months the abstracts arrive, just enough of them to form a typically sized volume. There are papers on music at the court of Henry VIII, on government and theocracy in Calvin's Geneva, on the regulation of space in the Palace of Versailles, on censorship of religious literature in Copenhagen, and more. Robin and Lucy decide to accept all the papers and assure the publisher that the book can be ready within two years. In the meantime, Robin's former supervisor, who is called Philip, has agreed to include a paper he gave some years ago at a different event on a loosely related topic; Lucy's supervisor has agreed to write a preface.

Six months later, the deadline for the full drafts is reached. Seven of the twelve drafts have arrived; three of these are significantly longer than the word limit set; one bears no resemblance to the abstract; one is almost unreadable. Of the five delinquents, three are apologetic and promise to do better; two have not replied to successive emails. There then begin many long months of haggling and heartache. Philip, rather more senior than either Robin or Lucy, seems unimpressed with their attempts to persuade him to amend his draft to focus more on the theme, and they back down. They have a nagging feeling that Helen's work is rather superficial and hasty, but do not know enough about Calvin's Geneva to challenge her. Two of the missing five drafts arrive; more emails are sent. Michael, under pressure from his university, withdraws his paper on Copenhagen in order to submit it to a 'top journal'. The two-year deadline comes and goes.

Eventually, Robin and Lucy decide that the papers in hand are all they are likely to have, and send the draft to the publisher. Their introduction, jointly written, is a baroquely inventive attempt to draw common themes from very disparate papers. After another year it appears in print, in an expensive hardback edition. Their publisher seems unwilling to invest in publicising it, so Robin and Lucy do what they can on social media. After two more years, it has been purchased by a handful of libraries; there have been no reviews. Robin has not written his book, and has taken on his third temporary teaching contract. Lucy has left the profession.

****

Although Robin and Lucy's tale is a fictional one, their experience embodies all the elements of a pervasive negative perception of the edited collection as a publishing format which has solidified in recent years. Two inexperienced editors convince an unenthusiastic publisher to accept a collection which contains essays only loosely connected, has little to say as a whole and answers no questions that are being asked. They are neither able to convince their contributors to produce their work in good time, nor to exert effective editorial control over the work that does materialise. Published years later than originally intended, the publisher, recognising its limitations, abandons the book to its fate, and it sinks without trace, leaving the editors with little to show for their heartache save their own copies. It is, however, not merely a story of the mishaps that beset most projects at one time or another, but a reflection of a latent but powerful general theory of the format.

The elements of this general theory may be stated as follows. Edited collections are widely suspected to contain work of a generally lower standard than scholarly journals, due largely to a less stringent regime of quality control; they are also supposed to be incoherent as volumes, being often no more than the sum of their parts; they take an inordinate amount of time from inception to completion, and are (it is thought) less visible to potential readers once published. By no means would all individual authors accept the critique. However, it is often taken as axiomatic that those who make important decisions in relation to hiring, promotion, tenure and funding do so agree, even if they themselves are also authors. To publish in or edit an essay collection (it is thought) is thus to risk being penalised for the format before even a word is read.

The extent to which the perception has spread is evident in a survey questionnaire of scholars in the humanities, completed in the autumn of 2018.[1] In the previous five years, more than half (56 per cent) of those who responded had been advised against publishing their work in edited collections. Although only 5 per cent reported formal institution-wide advice against the format, more than a quarter had been so advised by senior staff in their departments, and 13 per cent in formal training or career development settings. Advice from peers was also influential, both within the same institution (24 per cent) and elsewhere (27 per cent).[2]

---

[1] The humanities were defined in line with the qualification for Main Panel D of the UK's Research Excellence Framework, and as such excluded archaeology, law and architecture. A total of 363 complete (or usefully incomplete) responses were received, of which approximately half (181) were from the UK; a further 74 responses (20 per cent) were from the USA, 48 from elsewhere in Europe and 26 from Canada. Of these, 156 respondents (43 per cent) stated their primary discipline to be history; 79 (22 per cent) english language and literature; 27 (7 per cent) communication, cultural and media studies; 23 (6 per cent) modern languages and linguistics; 17 (5 per cent) for both classics and art and design; and 13 responses (4 per cent) for theology and religious studies. Responses for philosophy, music, film studies, and drama and dance each made up less than 3 per cent of the total.

[2] The pattern was largely consistent between different nations, with responses from the UK and the USA to this question (which between them formed nearly half of the results of the total) showing a comparable result (58 per cent).

This would be of no great significance if those receiving such advice thought it both justified in principle and beneficial for themselves in particular. However, the same survey revealed a marked misalignment between scholars' perceptions of (on the one hand) the best interests of their discipline, and what would best aid their own career, on the other. When thinking in terms of the health of their discipline, respondents were asked to choose one of four statements that best reflected their view. Were book chapters an 'essential part of scholarly publishing [which] add value of a different kind', or 'quite useful but secondary to journal articles'? Or, were they 'a waste of time [which] should be avoided'? Or did it not matter: was the key factor 'the quality and significance of what I write'? Just under a third of respondents thought chapters essential, one in four regarded them as secondary to journal articles; only a very few (4 per cent) thought that they should be avoided.

However, the responses were markedly different when the same question was framed in terms of career progression. Now, the choice of format was rather more important: where previously 38 per cent had thought that the publishing format was immaterial, now only 18 per cent believed so. Four times as many now thought chapters a waste of time, and 44 per cent thought them secondary to journal articles. Respondents were also asked to state what they thought was the general view of their peers on the same questions, and responses were markedly more negative again. Fully a quarter of respondents believed that their peers thought chapters should be avoided for the good of their careers, and another 46 per cent thought that their peers regarded them as secondary to journal articles.

This Element is the first extended critical examination of both perception and the reality of the edited collection of essays as a means of scholarly communication. I contend that the edited collection has a unique role to play in the communication of research both within and outside the universities. I also argue that, although all of the features of Robin and Lucy's experience are real, several have been overstated and none of them are inevitable. Section 2 examines the twentieth-century history of the format, and its many and changing functions in humanities publishing. Section 3 sets out the overall shape and the individual elements of the critique of the edited collection in more detail, and shows that few of them have firm basis in fact, and those that are so grounded are far from insoluble. The Conclusion looks to the future, and to an idea of scholarly community, much occluded, that the edited collection affords. But the recent history of that critique, and the manner in which it has been communicated, is in itself an instructive episode in the history of ideas.

Since it is some way outside my own specialism, I make no claim for the discipline of memetics in general, and the degree to which it matches psychological reality. Metaphorically, at least, the cluster of suppositions about the edited collection bears many of the marks of what Richard Dawkins termed a 'meme complex'.[3] The complex of individual ideas (or memes) about the edited collection have all functioned in a largely unexamined way, but with an unusual degree of 'memetic fitness' in the struggle of ideas to survive and spread. That fitness has perhaps been due to some of their structural features as ideas. They are simple and memorable: 'edited collections are to be avoided'; they are psychologically attractive (in that they appeal to basic instincts of professional self-preservation) and are also conducive to action (or, in this case, the active eschewing of certain choices of where to publish). All of these are features of memes most likely to survive, replicate and displace others in human subjects. There is a certain irony in the fact that the humanities, dedicated as they are to the critical examination of ideas, have internalised this particular complex of memes with little challenge or debate.

When did this 'crisis of the edited collection' begin? (How old, as it were, is this meme complex?) There are isolated pieces of evidence of scholarly concern dating back decades, such as that from the psychologist (and later pioneer of the Open Access (OA) movement) Stevan Harnad in 1986, who thought it 'folly . . . to bury what one takes to be good papers in edited conference volumes'.[4] In the humanities, the evidence is much less clear. Some of those I interviewed recalled advice against publishing their work in this format before the 2008 Research Assessment Exercise in the

---

[3] C. von Bülow, 'Mem', in J. Mittelstraß (ed.), *Enzyklopädie Philosophie und Wissenschaftstheorie* (2nd edition, volume 5, Springer, 2013), pp. 318–24.

[4] S. Harnad, 'On reviewing (and publishing in) edited interdisciplinary volumes', *Contemporary Psychology* 31 (5), 1986, 390.

UK (of which, more in Section 3). As an early career scholar, I myself was certainly advised by a senior colleague (in 2004) against editing such a volume on the grounds that they were poorly regarded and not widely read.

However, by virtue of their verbal transmission and anecdotal nature, the spread of these memes is hard to trace. Only after the middle of the first decade of the century do critiques and defences of the format begin to appear on the academic Web, in a trickle which became a steady flow after 2010. Little of this literature is formally published, although the last five years have seen a handful of studies in aspects of the issue. Much of it appears in the form of personal reflections from editors, publishers and authors,[5] and as career advice to early career scholars.[6] Criticisms of the genre are drawn from across the disciplines, but in particular from the social sciences; the genre has also had its defenders.

1.1 Definitions

Of what do we speak when we speak of the 'edited collection'? The term has been made to encompass a number of distinct although related forms of publication. Here I define it in terms of three criteria: its contents, the

---

[5] Examples not cited elsewhere include: M. E. Smith, 'Why are so many edited volumes worthless?', *Publishing Archaeology*, 26 August 2007, retrieved 1 May 2019 from http://publishingarchaeology.blogspot.com/2007/08/why-are-so-many-edited-volumes.html; A. Hacker, 'In defense of the edited book', *A Hacker's View*, 3 December 2013, retrieved 1 March 2019 from www.andreahacker.com/in-defense-of-the-edited-book/; M. Kremakova, 'What's so bad about book chapters? Nothing really', *The Sociological Imagination* (9 June 2016), retrieved 17 December 2019 from https://web.archive.org/web/20170626034643/http://sociologicalimagination.org/archives/18684.

[6] Examples not cited elsewhere include: K. Kelsky, 'Should I do an edited collection?', *The Professor Is In*, 24 July 2012, retrieved 1 June 2018 from http://theprofessorisin.com/2012/07/24/should-i-do-an-edited-collection/; C. Guerin, 'Journal article or book chapter?', *Doctoral Writing Special Interest Group* (1 May 2014), retrieved 1 August 2018 from https://doctoralwriting.wordpress.com/2014/05/01/journal-article-or-book-chapter/.

process by which it comes into being, and the form and manner in which it is presented.

I define an edited collection as a group of written outputs, of a length comparable to an article in a learned journal. They will have been written by different authors, although individual chapters may have more than one author. I therefore set aside the monograph, and also the relatively rare species of the jointly written book, even if its chapters are individually attributed to one or more authors. This definition also excludes the genres of encyclopaedia and dictionary, on grounds of length (but includes the various species of companions and handbooks, as explained later). Even though some individual contributions to such books are of a length comparable to an article, the majority are in general not.

Secondly, these books are the result of a set of distinctive processes. These collections must necessarily have one or more editors, with whom rests the decision of which contributions are included and which are not. They may very often themselves contribute a preface, introduction, conclusion or epilogue; these will most likely state the larger intellectual problem to which the chapters address themselves, draw out themes in common, reflect on dissonance between the chapters and set out the implications for the field in the future. They may well (but do not always) intervene to shape the individual chapters to address the theme, in consultation with the author.

It is in this activist editorial role that we see most clearly the difference between the edited collection and the genre of the conference proceeding. While edited collections as I define them quite often have their genesis in a conference of some sort, the conference proceeding functions as the final record of an event. In general, the conference proceeding model in which papers are submitted and peer reviewed in advance and published simultaneously with the event is rare in the humanities, although very common in other disciplines.[7] Even when (as is more common in the humanities), the publication takes place after the event, there is often a presumption that all

---

[7] For more on the rather indistinct line between the two genres, see *Open Access and Book Chapters* (British Academy, 2019). I myself acted as a consultant to the team producing this report.

papers given at the conference will be included, subject to some basic tests of quality. The papers were likely to have been intellectually complete at the time of the conference, and they will not substantially change between event and publication, although a shortened version may have been read in person. The edited collection, in contrast, often bears a more distant relationship with the event: some contributions are not included, and others are included that were not presented at the event. As there is a greater lapse of time between event and publication, the potential for change and development in the text itself is greater, under the direction of the editor(s). The event is merely one single step in a process of development of a coherent set of essays.

Thirdly, the edited collection is very clearly packaged as a coherent whole. It will have a title that defines its scope and ambition as a monograph will, and most likely will be treated the same as a monograph for marketing and sales purposes. It is on these grounds, therefore, that I set aside the genre of the special issue of a journal. Although it meets my first two criteria, the special issue is quite distinct in several ways. It is rarely packaged in as distinctive and as durable a way, and is rarely subject to quite the same expectations of coherence and comprehensiveness. The edited collection also has a finality, or at least a closedness, which contrasts with the more open-ended nature of a journal, the continuing record of the deliberation of a community of scholars. I shall return to the issue of visibility in Section 3.

1.2 Companions and Handbooks

There is a further genre of academic publishing which meets all of the criteria of my definition – and is included here – but has some particular features of note: the various series of what are generally labelled 'companions' or 'handbooks'. These may be distinguished from the encyclopaedia and the dictionary by virtue of the length of the contributions, which tends to be closer to that for a chapter or article. In general, their relation to their subject matter is distinctive. Rarely do they emerge from a conference or an open call for papers. Instead, the subject to be covered is tightly defined in advance, and contributions solicited to cover each aspect. Although the distinction is not absolute, handbooks and companions also tend to be directed to subjects that are already thought to be important; it is relatively rare that an emerging field of study is dealt with in this way.

In the course of writing this Element, I interviewed a number of humanities scholars and librarians.[8] One interviewee, a historian of modern Britain, thought the genre of handbooks or companions prone to a kind of intellectual conservatism – one that at its worst was an invitation to established scholars merely to restate their existing work in summary form rather than to break new ground. Although this is evidently a risk of the genre, it is often avoided, and such writings have been submitted to research assessment exercises such as the Research Excellence Framework in the UK, and received as world-leading research.[9] Chapters that are formative and others that are merely summative may well appear in the same volume. Even at their most conservative, these books are clearly quite distinct from the genre of the textbook, although they may well be used in teaching. (Indeed, the textbook genre is by no means as secure a feature of the humanities as in other disciplines, but to explore that further is beyond my scope.[10])

Compared to the edited volume at large, the companion and the handbook are relatively recent genres. The most well-established series of companions, from Cambridge University Press, was established in the late 1980s, beginning with figures in English literature (Shakespeare, Milton); volumes on the most significant philosophers began to appear in the early 1990s (Marx, Descartes and Plato among the early subjects). The series on music – dealing initially with individual composers and musical

---

[8] In total, nineteen individuals were interviewed in late 2018 and early 2019, among them historians, theologians, musicologists and librarians. All but one were UK-based; most were in university settings, of various types, while others were active scholars and teachers employed by other institutions. Some were senior scholars, some in mid-career and others were early career scholars.

[9] Research Excellence Framework 2014. *Overview Report by Main Panel D and Sub-panels 27 to 36*, retrieved 17 December 2019 from www.ref.ac.uk/2014/panels/paneloverviewreports/, p. 62.

[10] On the problematic category of the textbook for history, see L. Jordanova, *History in Practice* (Arnold, 2000), pp. 18–19.

instruments – began in 1992 with volumes on Chopin and on the violin. The series expanded in scope by the millennium to encompass the theatre, and literatures other than English; volumes on the Bible and Christian doctrine appeared in 1997; major theologians such as Dietrich Bonhoeffer and Karl Barth were also dealt with, and the figure of Jesus himself in 2001. The series has continued to grow ever since.

I distinguished earlier between companions and handbooks on the one hand, and dictionaries and encyclopaedias on the other hand, on the grounds of the length of contributions. That these meanings of these terms have only stabilised in the last three decades is shown by volumes such as the *Oxford Companion to the Theatre*, first published in 1951 and in its fourth edition in 1983, which despite the name has all the features of the dictionary/encyclopaedia. However, Oxford University Press began a series of handbooks in the more recent sense in the mid-1980s, beginning with medicine, but after the millennium expanding into areas of the humanities, beginning with philosophy, theology and religious studies and subsequently including works of history and musicology. The series now contains several hundred volumes. It was closely followed by the series of Blackwell companions (now Wiley-Blackwell), founded in the late 1980s but picking up speed in the mid-1990s. The British publisher Ashgate (which was acquired by Informa, parent company of Taylor and Francis, in 2015) also had a series of 'research companions'.[11] Begun in 2007, it continues under the Routledge imprint. Routledge had already an established handbook series, which began at much the same time and at the time of writing amounted to several hundred volumes, a significant proportion of which are in the humanities.

Finally, there are two genres of volume which share all the marks of the edited collection as I have defined it, but which I also set aside. I define an edited collection as one in which all (or nearly all) the content is written for the volume, or (at least) has not previously been published. There is a durable tradition of the republication in book form of the most significant

---

[11] 'Informa pays £20m for Ashgate Publishing', *The Bookseller*, 29 July 2015, retrieved on 7 March 2019 from www.thebookseller.com/news/informa-pays -20m-ashgate-publishing-308308.

recent articles on a particular topic, examples of which could be found from any time in the last sixty years at least. These have sometimes been labelled as 'readers' or 'anthologies', but not always so, and not all volumes badged as such contain whole papers, or indeed very recent ones. These volumes have come about for various reasons: because the articles first appeared in relatively obscure journals and deserve to be more accessible; because a topic has come to be seen as more important in recent years; or merely for the convenience of having them available in one volume. Although they sometimes perform some of the same functions as markers of the state of a field at a point in time, most of the elements of the critique of edited collections which I explore here do not apply, and so I set them aside.

The second genre that I exclude is the Festschrift. These collections of essays 'in honour of' or 'presented to' a senior scholar, also sometimes known as the 'liber amicorum', seem to share all the formal features of the edited collection: multiple contributors under the guidance of one or more editors, contributing pieces of writing which are in some sense connected. Unique to the format are various kinds of biographical sketches of the dedicatee, personal recollections, lists of publications, images of manuscripts, photographs, portraits and more. But it is the ambiguous, and indeed sometimes self-contradictory, nature of the connection between the chapters that often vitiates the success of the Festschrift.

The contributors to a Festschrift usually stand in some form of personal intellectual relationship with the dedicatee: former graduate students, colleagues, collaborators. But senior scholars have usually supervised and collaborated with many more scholars than can be accommodated in a single volume. The historian Susan Pedersen observed that the fascination of the Festschrift is not so much in the individual contributions but in what its inclusions and exclusions reveal, 'openly and almost innocently', about the recent history of a discipline and its current structures of power and influence.[12]

Since the primary purpose of the Festschrift is to form part of a particular kind of gift economy, the cumulative effect of the essays themselves is at best a secondary consideration, and at worst largely lost. When the dedicatee's work remained within a particular field of enquiry over a whole career, and/

---

[12] S. D. Pedersen, 'Festschriftiness', *London Review of Books* 33 (19), 31–2.

or the contributors themselves continued in that field, the editors stand
a chance of creating a volume in which the essays cohere thematically. If
not, editors have on occasion chosen to focus on one aspect of a scholar's
work to achieve coherence. Among the three Festschrifts prepared for the
historian Geoffrey Elton, it is arguably the volume that is focused particularly
on Tudor law and government that coheres most clearly.[13] In cases where the
dedicatee ranged widely, the result is often a collection of essays that he or she
might find interesting, but relate to each other hardly at all.[14] Some have also
noted the tendency for the Festschrift to become 'a permanent resting place
for their otherwise unpublishable or at least difficult to publish papers'.[15] It is
for this reason, as the publisher Irving Horowitz argued, that publishers have
often regarded such volumes as a 'discharge of unavoidable and costly
obligation to famous authors presented in the category of a non-book'.[16]
To be clear, my argument is not that such incoherence is inevitable in
a Festschrift – many examples show that it is not – or that such incoherence
(where it does occur) renders them worthless. We should not apply the same
criteria of coherence to these volumes, since it is not their primary purpose,
but it is on this criterion that I shall place significant stress in the rest of my
argument. As that is the case, the Festschrift is set aside.

2 Pasts

This section explores the history of the edited collection in the twentieth
century, as a means of drawing out the particular purposes it has often

---

[13] C. Cross, D. Loades and J. Scarisbrick (eds), *Law and Government under the Tudors* (Cambridge University Press, 1983). The editors were Elton's first three graduate students in the University of Cambridge.

[14] For an example, see A. G. Soble, 'Review of "Fact and Value: Essays on Ethics and Metaphysics for Judith Jarvis Thomson"', *Essays in Philosophy*, 4 (1), article 5, at https://commons.pacificu.edu/eip/vol4/iss1/5/.

[15] E. Tulving, 'Are There 256 Different Kinds of Memory?' in J. S. Nairne (ed.), *The Foundations of Remembering: Essays in Honor of Henry L. Roedinger, III* (Psychology Press, 2007), pp. 39–52, at p. 39.

[16] I. L. Horowitz, *Communicating Ideas: The Politics of Scholarly Publishing*, 2nd edition (Routledge, 2017), chapter 20.

served. I dwell on a group of particular case studies, each of them unique, but with some common features. One of these is the life and work of the British composer Benjamin Britten. I also examine two genres particular to history: the multi-author (and often multi-volume) general histories first associated with Cambridge University Press, and (secondly) the institutional history. The section then examines some key trends in the recent history of British universities and of academic publishing, and the ways in which changing contexts altered the role the edited collection played. Finally, by means of two further case studies, I suggest that the increased importance of the edited collection in the formation of new disciplines is in part a function of those publishing trends. I begin, however, with theology, and an extended examination of twentieth-century Anglican theology in particular, as a means of introducing the issues.

Generalisation is difficult, of course, since every edited volume has its own story, of a discipline at a point in time and of a group of scholars, each with their particular perspectives. Some of these volumes are motivated purely by the developmental logic of a particular line of enquiry. Others are more consciously intended as interventions to shape, or even disrupt, the nature of the discipline itself; to force an acknowledgement of new methods, theoretical frameworks or subjects that had hitherto been marginal. Others still have an overtly political purpose (in the broadest sense of the term), to bring expert insight to a larger issue of public concern, or to push a discipline to address that issue. They are also inevitably themselves shaped by the national contexts from which they grow; my case studies here (as well as in Section 3) are primarily from the UK, with some comment on the wider Anglo-American and European situations, but scholars in India or Japan (for instance) might well tell quite different stories.

Primarily, my examples are chosen to draw out the fundamentally *conversational* nature of the edited collection. Born themselves often from ongoing interactions among groups of scholars, edited collections often display those conversations, with all the elements of consonance and dissonance that are entailed. In their turn, these volumes often become points of reference in the continuing conversations within the discipline. Musicology and theology are particular cases in that they have ongoing relationships with institutions and professions outside the academy – namely, the music profession and religious organisations – on the practices of which they dwell and to which they aspire to speak. Examples might be produced from other areas, for instance, in the intersection between contemporary history, politics and government.[17] But even in areas of the humanities with less obvious external readers, the edited collection still facilitates conversations among scholars – which surely must be an aim in common – in a unique way.

2.1 Theology

Modern Anglican theology has had a long tradition of groups of scholars coming together to address issues that cut across the discipline as a whole. In the late 1950s, Alec Vidler was fellow and dean of King's College, Cambridge, and held one of the commanding heights of the discipline in England, the editorship of the journal *Theology*. Vidler had been asked by younger colleagues in the divinity faculty to convene a group to address a dissatisfaction with the general state of Anglican theology. His memoirs record regular meetings of a dozen scholars at which papers were read and discussed.[18] After a long weekend conference, the group was convinced that there were fundamental issues in theology that needed to be faced; the result was *Soundings: Essays Concerning Christian Understanding*, published in 1962 by Cambridge University Press.[19] Its effect in the universities was far-reaching. In 1965, a Cambridge graduate seminar was established in Christology (the theology of the person of Jesus Christ in particular), to work through some of the issues that had been raised. Although the two volumes had only one contributor in common, the resulting collection of essays – *Christ, Faith and History: Cambridge Studies in Christology* (1972)[20] – acknowledged its debt to *Soundings*.

[17] See, for instance A. Seldon (ed.), *The Blair Effect. The Blair Government, 1997–2001* (Little, Brown, 2001), sponsored by the Institute of Contemporary British History.

[18] A. Vidler, *Scenes from a Clerical Life: An Autobiography* (Collins, 1977), pp. 176–8.

[19] A. Vidler (ed.), *Soundings: Essays Concerning Christian Understanding* (Cambridge University Press, 1962), pp. ix–xii.

[20] S. W. Sykes and J. P. Clayton (eds), *Christ, Faith and History: Cambridge Studies in Christology* (Cambridge University Press, 1972).

Soundings was in the planning as the centenary approached of another controversial volume of English theological essays, *Essays and Reviews* (1860), a bid by a group of scholars, mostly clergy, for the freedom to engage with the revolutionary new findings of biblical criticism.[21] For the *Soundings* group, the issues were more philosophical, but Vidler, in his preface, explicitly set *Soundings* in a line of succession from *Essays and Reviews*, at least in character. In turn there appeared *New Soundings: Essays on Developing Tradition* (1997), a conscious echo of Vidler's book. It too was the work of a group of scholars who had taken time and 'stepped back from the ongoing life of the Church, viewed its preoccupations ... this has, perhaps, become something of a tradition in itself'.[22]

Also in Vidler's line of succession was *Lux Mundi* (1889), officially censured by the Church just as was *Essays and Reviews*.[23] The twelve authors, all of them Anglicans and all of them clergy, had been together in Oxford between 1875 and 1885, a number of them meeting each year as a 'Holy Party' for several days of study and discussion.[24] They wrote as Christian ministers, accepting the Christian faith as still sufficient as a means of interpreting human existence. But in a time of intellectual and social transformation, there were required 'great changes in the outlying departments of theology, where it is linked on to other sciences, and ... some general restatement of its claim and meaning'.[25]

---

[21] P. Hinchliff, *Frederick Temple, Archbishop of Canterbury: A Life* (Clarendon Press, 1998), pp. 59–89.

[22] A. Chandler, 'Preface', in S. Platten, G. James and A. Chandler (eds), *New Soundings: Essays on Developing Tradition* (Darton, Longman and Todd, 1997), pp. vii–viii.

[23] On the controversy over the two books, see O. Chadwick, *The Victorian Church: Part Two: 1860–1901* (A. & C. Black, 1970), pp. 75–90, 101–4.

[24] On the making of *Lux Mundi*, see G. Rowell, 'Historical retrospect: *Lux Mundi* 1889', in R. Morgan (ed.), *The Religion of the Incarnation: Anglican Essays in Commemoration of* Lux Mundi (Bristol Classical Press, 1989), pp. 205–17.

[25] C. Gore (ed.), *Lux Mundi: A Series of Studies in the Religion of the Incarnation* (14th edition, John Murray, 1895), p. vii–viii.

Lux Mundi has come to be regarded as a milestone in theological history.[26] It also served as a model. On its own centenary in 1989 it attracted not one but two further edited collections, both reflecting on its legacy and the current state of the debate over the issues it raised. Both volumes set themselves the task of the kind of overarching assessment of the field that *Lux Mundi* had essayed, and adopted a similar structure. Both emerged after several years' deliberation, in one case a whole decade. As with *Lux Mundi*, the authors of *The Religion of the Incarnation* had all been connected with the University of Oxford, and all but three remained so.[27] The contributors to *Keeping the Faith* in contrast were not all Anglicans, and not all from the UK, and as such had less opportunity to interact in person save for a week-long conference, although debate and mutual refinement continued by correspondence. They saw themselves as in 'theological fellowship' with the *Lux Mundi* men, an explicitly Christian articulation of a sense of community that was latent more widely.[28]

At several times in the last century, then, groups of Anglican theologians came together to address the discipline as a whole, in volumes that have themselves become models to emulate, and landmarks against which scholars could triangulate in changed conditions. But it was also the case that Anglican theology in England, intentionally or not, was part of broader conversations with readers outside the universities, with other disciplines, and with the nation at large.

Possibly the single most controversial work of English theology of the seventies was *The Myth of God Incarnate* (1977), edited by John Hick, then professor of theology in the University of Birmingham.[29] Its seven

---

[26] See the periodisation employed in M. Ramsey, *From Gore to Temple: The Development of Anglican Theology between* Lux Mundi *and the Second World War, 1889–1939* (Longmans, 1960).

[27] R. Morgan, 'Preface', in Morgan (ed.), *The Religion of the Incarnation*, pp. xiv–xvi.

[28] G. Wainwright, 'Preface', in G. Wainwright (ed.), *Keeping the Faith: Essays to Mark the Centenary of* Lux Mundi (Society for Promoting Christian Knowledge, 1989), pp. xix–xxv, at p. xxiii.

[29] J. Hick (ed.), *The Myth of God Incarnate* (SCM Press, 1977).

contributors were theologians from universities and Anglican theological colleges in Oxford, Cambridge and Birmingham. Two of them were, or had been, holders of the regius chairs of divinity in Oxford and Cambridge. Two had contributed to *Christ, Faith and History*. The authors were motivated by what they perceived to be the need for a fundamental reorientation in Christology. Like *Soundings*, the book had emerged through a sequence of meetings, five over three years. Even more so than *Soundings* (over which the public controversy was considerable), it reached far beyond the universities, and the dispute it generated was a significant moment in recent theological history. The book sold some 30,000 copies in its first eight months.[30]

The far-reaching implications of the argument both inside and outside the academy prompted a rapid response, including several further sets of essays of varying characters. One, a form of rebuttal, was from a group including both bishops and academics including the Lady Margaret Professor of Divinity at Oxford, John Macquarrie; *The Truth of God Incarnate* was published in an inexpensive edition by a religious trade press within weeks, and has the character of a set of review articles.[31] The following year, Hick and his fellow essayist Michael Goulder of the University of Birmingham brought together the group with some of their critics. Macquarrie, who had been so incensed by the book that it had ended up in his wastepaper basket, apparently declined an invitation to take part, but another of the *Truth* group, Brian Hebblethwaite, fellow and dean of Queen's College, Cambridge, did not.[32] This expanded group met in a sequence of ten meetings over two days; some of them private, some of them debates attended by a hundred or more members of the public. The result was *Incarnation and Myth: The Debate Continued* (1979), an arrangement of the participants' original papers and responses to them. Meanwhile another group of scholars in Oxford had begun to meet to discuss the issues

---

[30] M. Goulder (ed.), *Incarnation and Myth: The Debate Continued* (SCM Press, 1979).

[31] M. Green (ed.), *The Truth of God Incarnate* (Inter-Varsity Press, 1977).

[32] M. Green, *Adventure of Faith: Reflections on Fifty Years of Christian Service* (Zondervan, 2001), p. 141; Goulder, *Incarnation and Myth*, p. viii.

raised by *Myth*, and to find a way of expressing its thrust more positively, the result being the essays in *God Incarnate: Story and Belief* (1981).[33]

Each of these volumes, then, was an attempt of a group of theologians to speak to sections of the discipline but also to the contemporary Church, while a significant lay readership, without access to university libraries and thus journals, were able to listen in. There has also been a related and equally durable genre of edited volume, in which scholars and religious leaders speak, as it were, to the nation directly, on social and economic issues. Borne of a sense of political and social turbulence was *Christianity and the Crisis* (1933), its thirty-two contributors drawn together by the Anglican priest and Christian socialist, Percy Dearmer. It proceeded from the theology of human existence and the nature of a Christian society – for the assumption was that this was the natural state of English life – to practical matters of international relations, education, economics, the family, work and leisure. The authors included economists, political theorists, a university vice-chancellor, philosophers and others from outside both the Church and the academy.[34]

Among the contributors to *Christianity and the Crisis* were both archbishops of the Church of England, one of whom – William Temple, of York – later convened the so-called Malvern Conference of 1941, the papers of which were published. Looking forward to the end of the war, the conference brought figures such as T. S. Eliot and Dorothy L. Sayers together with members of Parliament, clergy and theologians to work out 'what are the fundamental facts of the new society, and how Christian thought can be shaped to play a leading part in the reconstruction'.[35] The degree to which this model retained a valency is evident in *On Rock or Sand? Firm Foundations for Britain's Future* (2015), edited by Temple's successor at York, John

[33] A. E. Harvey (ed.), *God Incarnate: Story and Belief* (Society for Promoting Christian Knowledge, 1981).

[34] P. Dearmer (ed.), *Christianity and the Crisis* (Victor Gollancz, 1933).

[35] W. Temple, *Malvern 1941: The Life of the Church and the Order of Society: Being the Proceedings of the Archbishop of York's Conference* (Longmans, Green and Co., 1941), p. ix.

Sentamu.[36] Based on a series of private colloquia at Sentamu's official residence which began shortly after the financial crisis of 2008, it included clergy and theologians, politicians, economists and senior figures from local government and the voluntary sector. Although squarely aimed at a general readership, it directly references Temple's Malvern conference as its inspiration.

One particular strand of interventions has been on the relationship between the established Church and the nation, as that relationship came under increased scrutiny. *Church and Politics Today: The Role of the Church of England in Contemporary Politics*[37] appeared in 1985, in a climate of increased tension between Church and state which was both symbolised and heightened by the dispute between Archbishop Robert Runcie and Prime Minister Margaret Thatcher over the memory of the Falklands War. Edited by the political scientist George Moyser, it brought together clergy, university-based theologians and others actively involved in politics, including one MP. That the particular question of the establishment of the Church of England remains unsettled was evident in *The Established Church: Past, Present and Future* (2011), edited by three historians from the University of Oxford, and drawing together historians, theologians and political scientists, most (although not all) of whom were also from Oxford.[38]

The edited collection, then, has been a means of brokering conversations of all kinds in Anglican theology. Some were among professional theologians; others between those within the academy and those outside who were more directly involved in the contemporary life of the Church of England; others again were between theologians and scholars from other disciplines and professionals in other spheres, as theology and ethics met with economics and politics. Some of the same patterns may be observed in another area of twentieth-century scholarship, on the work of Benjamin Britten.

---

[36] (SPCK, 2015).

[37] G. Moyser (ed.), *Church and Politics Today: The Role of the Church of England in Contemporary Politics* (T. & T. Clark, 1985).

[38] M. Chapman, J. Maltby and W. Whyte (eds), *The Established Church: Past, Present and Future* (Mowbray, 2011).

2.2 Benjamin Britten

In 1952, there appeared a volume of essays on the English composer Benjamin Britten, subtitled *A Commentary on His Works by a Group of Specialists*.[39] The young freelance music critic Donald Mitchell, one of the two editors, recalled that the book had been designed as a corrective to a widespread critical hostility to Britten's work, a demand that his music be taken seriously. The book was widely attacked for a marked lack of critical distance in some chapters, and Britten himself, although flattered, felt somewhat 'like a small and harmless rabbit being cut up by a lot of grubby schoolboys'.[40] But the contributors were serious enough: the composers Lennox Berkeley and George Malcolm; performers including the conductors Norman del Mar and Boyd Neel; and one of Britten's foremost interpreters (and his life partner), the tenor Peter Pears. Also included were musicologists including Hans Redlich (later professor of music at the University of Manchester), Erwin Stein, and Mitchell's co-editor, Hans Keller. Scholars, composers and performers came together to make the case for the music of a contemporary, a case now largely acknowledged as won.

That this interweaving of critical and academic voices happened outside a university context (and was not published by an academic press) was in part a function of the relative youth of musicology as a subject of formalised study. In his survey of the discipline, Joseph Kerman named both Stein and Keller as pioneers in the UK, and since the 1950s, musicology has developed a secure institutional base within the universities that it did not have at the time anywhere save for Germany.[41] But like theology, music is not only studied for its own sake but as part of the continual interplay of composition, performance, recording and listening. The symposial method was already established before the Mitchell and Keller volume. Britten himself had contributed to such a volume about his 1946 opera *The Rape of Lucretia*, in which he, his librettist Ronald Duncan, designer John Piper and producer

---

[39] D. Mitchell and H. Keller (eds), *Benjamin Britten: A Commentary on His Works from a Group of Specialists* (Rockliff, 1952).

[40] H. Carpenter, *Benjamin Britten: A Biography* (Faber, 1992), pp. 315–16.

[41] J. Kerman, *Musicology* (Fontana, 1985), p. 27.

Eric Crozier came together to reflect on the making of the work, since it diverged significantly from the grand opera model.[42] It also included an extensive analysis of the music by the writer and critic Henry Boys, a contemporary from Britten's time at the Royal College of Music. Both Britten and Pears were contributors to a 1959 volume on the music of Henry Purcell, as performers and (in Britten's case) a realiser of the keyboard accompaniment to Purcell's songs. While Pears was less than critical – '[t]here is really no need to probe; it is enough to love ... our incomparable Orpheus Britannicus' – Britten's contribution was more substantial, and the volume includes key early essays in the rediscovery of Purcell's music and its context.[43] In both cases, scholars, composers and performers came together to work out the significance of the works and the means of realising them.

Britten died in 1976, and the surge of scholarly interest that followed his death was supported by the availability of his papers and manuscripts in the Britten–Pears Library and Archive. It was and is situated in Aldeburgh, Britten and Pears' home, part of the continuing milieu that included the Aldeburgh Festival that the two men had founded. And over the next decade, although there was yet no specialist journal of 'Britten Studies', the study of his work blossomed, in journal articles, monographs and edited collections. The series of Cambridge Opera Handbooks (which began in 1981) soon covered *Peter Grimes* (1983), *The Turn of the Screw* (1985) and *Death in Venice* (1987). Although much of the material on *Grimes* had previously been published, the later two were largely new, with historico-biographical essays on the making of the works, analyses of the music, and assessments of its performance history and subsequent reception.

There were also two more general companions, which acknowledged the formal precedent of Mitchell and Keller's 1952 volume, and its impact at the time in giving Britten's work a musicological respectability. *The Britten Companion*, published by Faber in 1984, was edited by the prolific young composer and writer Christopher Palmer, and brought performers and

---

[42] R. Duncan (ed.), *The Rape of Lucretia: A Symposium* (Bodley Head, 1948).

[43] I. Holst (ed.), *Henry Purcell, 1659–1695: Essays on His Music* (Oxford University Press, 1959), Pears quotation at p. 6.

composers together with poets, university-based scholars and others who had worked with Britten, including his former music assistant Rosamund Strode, who at the time of writing was custodian of his manuscripts at Aldeburgh.[44] The subsequent Cambridge companion, published in 1999 and edited by Mervyn Cooke, composer and lecturer in music at the University of Nottingham, exhibits similarities and discontinuities.[45] With some exceptions, notably Donald Mitchell, few of the contributors could now draw on direct professional experience of working with Britten during his lifetime. The focus of some of the essays had also shifted with the priorities of the academy, with a notably clearer apprehension of historical context afforded by increased distance. However, although the proportion of the contributors in university posts had risen, still several were performers, archivists or librarians for performing organisations, or freelance writers and critics; the same sense of a conversation between scholars and practitioners that had marked the Mitchell and Keller volume remained.

2.3 Institutional Histories

So far I have discussed one whole discipline (Anglican theology) and the treatment of one particular subject within a discipline (Britten and musicology). I move now to consider two particular ways of imagining such volumes, both from the discipline of history. Among publishing formats for historians, the reputation of corporate or institutional histories has perhaps suffered from some of the more antiquarian and self-congratulatory examples of the genre, made for a boardroom coffee table. But there is a durable tradition, certainly in the UK, of scholarly treatments of the history of a particular institution, and often these have multiple contributors. The two oldest university presses in the UK, those of Oxford and Cambridge universities, both have their official histories. While that for Cambridge has a single author, the four-volume history of Oxford University Press is comprised of contributions from some sixty-nine

---

[44] C. Palmer (ed.), *The Britten Companion* (Faber, 1984), pp. 13–14.

[45] M. Cooke (ed.), *The Cambridge Companion to Benjamin Britten* (Cambridge University Press, 1999), p. 4.

contributors.[46] Other examples are numerous, but these histories themselves have histories, being the composite work of many individuals in institutional and geographical contexts. One example is the particularly English subgenre of the cathedral history.

Several of the English cathedral churches date their foundation, or at least the building of their current structures, to the Anglo-Norman period, and so, as the end of the twentieth century approached, there was a crop of cathedral histories, some of them tied to nine-hundredth or other anniversary commemorations. First off the mark was York Minster, with a volume of essays published in 1977 by Clarendon Press. The initiative had come from the dean and chapter (the governing body of the minster), against a background of growing interest in its archaeology and its monuments. An initial editorial committee included Owen Chadwick, regius professor of modern history at Cambridge (and also a priest and person of some influence within the Church of England), who also contributed a chapter. But the volume was also a local affair, being eventually edited by Gerald Aylmer, the first professor of history in the still young University of York (founded in 1963), and Reginald Cant, canon chancellor of the minster.[47] Most of the other contributors were university-based scholars connected either with Cambridge or York; the early architecture was covered by Eric A. Gee of the Royal Commission on Historical Monuments, which was based in the city; the chapter on the minster library was by C. B. L. Barr, of the university library, in the custody of which the minster library was kept.

Since then, there has been a crop of similar volumes as the other ancient cathedrals have followed suit, all with more or less the same characteristics. Most of these volumes had some sort of connection with a local university and involvement from writers associated with the cathedral itself. They have tended to encompass several disciplinary perspectives: national and local history, musicology, archaeology, bibliography and the history of art and architecture. The combination of those perspectives has varied,

---

[46] S. Eliot (ed.), *The History of Oxford University Press* (four volumes, Oxford University Press, 2013–17).

[47] G. Aylmer and R. Cant (eds), *A History of York Minster* (Clarendon Press, 1977); see the preface, pp. v–vi.

however, and the balance between university and city also. Oxford University Press published the volume for Canterbury Cathedral, the principal church in England, in 1995. More than a decade in the planning, the impetus had come both from the press and from Donald Coggan, archbishop of Canterbury until 1980.[48] All three editors were connected with Canterbury, including the historian Patrick Collinson, regius professor in Cambridge but formerly professor at the University of Kent. However, the team of contributors was overwhelmingly professional and drawn from several universities.

By contrast, the 1994 volume for Chichester was composed of work from a more diverse and locally focused group. It was edited by the cathedral archivist, Mary Hobbs, with the assistance of a historian at the West Sussex Institute of Higher Education (now the University of Chichester), Andrew Foster, who also wrote the chapter on the post-Reformation cathedral. The deputy county archivist (in whose care much of the historic archive rests) dealt with the cathedral's archives and its antiquaries, and Hobbs herself with the library. The chapters on the medieval and early modern cathedral were from specialists, as were those on the architecture and on the cathedral's art. The twentieth-century chapters, in contrast, were by clergy with a connection with the cathedral.[49] The cathedral history, then, has been a meeting point of institutional history and the local history of a city with religious history more broadly, and the concerns of historians of architecture, music, art and of the book. The collaborative volume has been found to be a useful means of brokering that interchange.

2.4 The 'General History'

At the very end of the nineteenth century, Cambridge University Press spotted an opportunity, the taking of which brought into existence one of the most characteristic genres of British historical publishing: the multi-author, multi-volume general history. There had been an increase in the popularity of history, in the universities and among the educated general

---

[48] 'Editors' preface', in P. Collinson, N. Ramsay and M. Sparks (eds), *A History of Canterbury Cathedral* (Oxford University Press, 1995), p. vii.

[49] M. Hobbs (ed.), *Chichester Cathedral: An Historical Survey* (Phillimore, 1994).

public, as a literary exercise and as a means of understanding contemporary politics and international affairs. Here, the press saw a new market. The planning of what became the *Cambridge Modern History* began in 1896, led by Lord Acton, although he did not live to see even the first volume completed. Acton drew up a general plan with the intention of involving 'the largest number of available writers, inviting every English historian who is competent, to contribute at least a chapter', and a list was drawn up. Its twenty volumes, with contributions from no fewer than 160 scholars, appeared between 1902 and 1912.[50] The *Cambridge Medieval History*, initially under the direction of J. B. Bury, was published between 1911 and 1936, the *Cambridge Ancient History* between 1924 and 1939, and the series on English literature appeared between 1907 and 1916 in fourteen volumes.[51] Similar series followed, including on India (from 1922), British foreign policy (in a compact three volumes) and the British Empire (from 1929).

The appearance of the first set of Cambridge Histories was indicative of a particular moment in the discipline, of both realism and (in retrospect) remarkable overconfidence. It was realistic, in that both the press and Acton recognised that the creation of such works was beyond any one individual; the discipline had reached a point of methodological precision that there could be no equivalent of Gibbon or Carlyle. Even then, the first thought of the Syndics (those who directed the affairs of the press) had still been to aim for a 'History of the World', which was reduced to the only slightly more manageable period since the Renaissance. Within that reduced scope, Acton rather improbably believed that 'nearly all the evidence that will ever appear is accessible now' and so the profession was within sight of 'the final stage in the conditions of historical

[50] G. N. Clark, 'The origin of the Cambridge Modern History', *Cambridge Historical Journal* 8 (2), 1945, 57–64.

[51] P. J. Rhodes, 'The Cambridge Ancient History', *Histos* 3, 1999, 18–26; P. A. Linehan, 'The making of the Cambridge Medieval History', *Speculum* 57 (3), 1982, 463–94. See also D. McKitterick, *A history of Cambridge University Press: Vol. 3: New Worlds for Learning, 1873–1972* (Cambridge University Press, 2004), pp. 154–64, 261, 274–5.

learning'.[52] Acton's confidence was shown to be misplaced: the first volume of the revised *Cambridge Ancient History* appeared in 1961, only two decades after the last volume of the first series. Already in 1945, there was a plan to revise Acton's modern history, since 'the accepted idea of general history has changed'.[53]

The general preface of the *Oxford History of the British Empire* (1998–9) gives some sense of the changed conditions that forced the revision of these histories in each generation or two.[54] The preceding Cambridge History had appeared between 1929 and 1959 just as the empire itself was being dismantled at remarkable speed. Where the earlier work had neglected the histories of Asia and Africa, and concentrated on constitutional history and that of government, the Oxford History set its sights wider, on the social and economic impact of the empire, and on those under its dominance, as well as of a UK made of four nations. In some cases where a series unfolded over many years, it could be criticised as outdated before it was even completed. The revised *Cambridge Ancient History* (begun in 1961) was itself a widening of scope when compared to the first series, but by 1999, while the work on it continued, that widening already appeared too conservative even to one of its contributors; so much so, in fact, that there had also appeared (in 1998, from the same press) a *Cambridge Illustrated History of Ancient Greece* with a rather more radical programme.[55] As one historian has observed, 'those Cambridge Histories fared best and reached port least scathed which travelled fastest'. Others, the *Medieval History* among them, 'ran aground and, like its nippier *Economic* sibling in due course, presented the scholarly world with a sitting target'.[56] Volume 7 of the *Cambridge Economic History of Europe* appeared in 1978,

---

[52] Acton's letter to prospective contributors, as quoted at Rhodes, 'Cambridge Ancient History', p. 19.

[53] M. Bentley, *Modernizing England's Past: English Historiography in the Age of Modernism, 1870–1970* (Cambridge University Press, 2005), p. 112.

[54] W. R. Louis, 'Preface', in P. J. Marshall, *The Eighteenth Century* (Oxford University Press, 1998), pp. vii–ix.

[55] Rhodes, 'Cambridge Ancient History', p. 23.

[56] Linehan, 'Cambridge Medieval History', p. 493.

a quarter of a century after volume 2 had appeared: for one reviewer, it was 'some enormous ghastly relict whose survival into the present is turning into a sad and heavy embarrassment . . . there is nothing in the originally-planned format to justify retaining it now and many, many intellectual reasons for changing it.'[57]

To these critiques was added in the mid-1990s another, more fundamental, one, as historians in the UK were gripped by controversy over the implications of 'postmodernity' for the discipline.[58] At least one scholar thought the postmodern challenge touched the general history as a genre, such that a defence was required.[59] At its extreme, the denial of any hope of objectivity in historical writing cast doubt on the validity of the whole exercise, since in a multi-authored work there was neither objectivity in each author, nor a single intellect which could itself be placed in its context and thus worked with (or against) on those terms. Yet the format survived the controversy and continues in strength. The contrast between the first Cambridge Histories and their counterparts a century later is not so much in format but in the magnification applied. Acton's modern history covered the whole history of Europe over 400 years in twenty volumes; the two complementary series on Anglicanism and on the Protestant dissenting tradition, recently completed, between them occupy ten.[60]

2.5 The Recent Past: Technological and Institutional Change

So far in this section, I have drawn out some of the characteristic roles which the edited collection has played within the academic world: roles which may be observed being played for most of the twentieth century. The last two to three decades, however, have seen significant changes in the whole

---

[57] A. S. Milward in the *English Historical Review* 94 (373), 1979, 888–9.

[58] A sense of the debate may be gained from R. J. Evans, *In Defence of History* (Granta, 1997).

[59] Rhodes, 'Cambridge Ancient History', pp. 24–6.

[60] R. Strong (general editor), *The Oxford History of Anglicanism* (Oxford University Press, 2017–18); T. Larsen and M. Noll (general editors), *The Oxford History of Protestant Dissenting Traditions* (Oxford University Press, 2017–18).

institutional and technological context in which scholars in all disciplines work, each of which have affected the prospects of the edited collection. The general expansion of higher education in Europe and North America has necessarily increased the supply of research that might be published, or (to look at the question another way) increased the demand for publishing services. To take one discipline in particular: the Institute of Historical Research (part of the University of London) recorded fewer than 1,000 teachers of history in UK universities in the early 1960s, a figure that had increased to nearly 3,000 in 2008.[61] Comparable figures from the Higher Education Statistics Agency show a continuing rise, such that the figure in 2017 was approaching 3,500. Also in the UK, the number of PhD degrees awarded in history rose from fewer than 250 in 1995 to more than 700 in 2017.[62] The story of other individual disciplines will vary, as some wax while others wane, but the general trend is clear, of an increase in the number of scholars who wish (or are required) to publish.

This rise in the number of persons professionally engaged to teach and write has been accompanied by an increase in the volume of published work. Data from the British Library, derived from the British National Bibliography (BNB), provided listings of all titles for theology and religious studies published in the UK from 1950 to 2015. In the five years from 1950, the BNB recorded some 4,921 books (monographs and edited volumes); by the late 1980s, the figure had doubled; in the five years from 2010, it had reached 13,527, nearly a three-fold increase in sixty years.[63]

---

[61] Institute of Historical Research, 'Teachers of history numbers', *Making History: The Changing Face of the Profession in Britain* (2008), retrieved 3 April 2019 from www.history.ac.uk/makinghistory/resources/statistics/teachers.html.

[62] B. Waddell, 'Historians, PhDs and jobs, 1995–96 to 2017/18', *The Many-Headed Monster* (7 March 2019), retrieved 3 April 2019 from https://manyheadedmon ster.wordpress.com/2019/03/07/historians-phds-and-jobs-1995-96-to-2017-18/.

[63] The criterion for inclusion in this data was a Dewey decimal classification in the range 200 to 299. P. Webster, 'New British Library metadata for theology and church history' *Webstory* (4 June 2015), retrieved 3 April 2019 from https://peterwebster.me/2015/06/04/new-british-library-metadata-for-theology-and-church-history/.

By no means all the books included in the BNB numbers were academic in nature, but a similar story can be told from more narrowly curated data from the Bibliography of British and Irish History (BBIH).[64] In the early 1960s, the BBIH recorded approximately 1,000 monographs per year, and between 1,500 and 2,000 journal articles. In the early 1980s, monographs consistently numbered between 1,700 and 2,000 per year, and articles between 2,200 and 2,600. By the period 2011 to 2015, the annual average number of new monographs was 3,600, more than a three-fold increase in fifty years.[65] In the same period, just over 28,000 journal articles were recorded, an average of 5,600 each year, nearly three times that in the early 1960s. Even allowing for the fact that the BBIH's coverage has become more comprehensive since the 1990s, the growth is striking.

Viewed in isolation, these trends might suggest the advent of a golden age of the monograph. However, in recent years, the tenor of discussion of academic monograph publishing has been much more in terms of decline and crisis. While such talk of a crisis of the monograph needs critical examination, it is clear that, over the long term, the rising number of individual titles occurred alongside a precipitous collapse in the sales of each individual book.[66] Print runs of between 2,000 and 3,000 or more were relatively common in the 1970s; the figure by the first decade of the new century was closer to 400 or 500, and has fallen further since, to 200 or fewer.[67] Even allowing for the undoubted existence of much unsold stock

---

[64] My thanks are due to my former colleagues Simon Baker and Peter Salt of the BBIH for their assistance in providing data not otherwise publicly available, and in answering my queries about it. Thanks are also due to the Royal Historical Society under whose aegis the data has been collected from the outset, and to its publisher, Brepols.

[65] This rising trend in the number of book titles (including edited collections) published is confirmed across several (although not all) humanities and social science disciplines in the UK by the analysis in G. Crossick, *Monographs and Open Access: A Report to HEFCE* (Higher Education Funding Council for England, 2015), p. 21.

[66] See, for instance, the relatively sanguine analysis at Crossick, *Monographs*, pp. 21–2.

[67] Michael Jubb, *Academic Books and Their Future: A Report to the AHRC and the British Library* (The Academic Book of the Future, 2017), p. 12.

from those larger runs, the trend is unmistakeable.[68] Although the costs of publishing were brought down in the same period by the digitisation of the typesetting process, it was not enough to offset the effect of falling sales. As such, a feasible business model has evolved: hardback books with minimal design and relatively low production standards, very short print runs (or print on demand), with prices as high as £100, aimed exclusively at the small group of academic libraries collecting in that particular specialism. I shall return to the issue of price and library purchasing in Section 3.

One of the perennial features of academic life, and not only in the UK, is bouts of worry from time to time about the supposed baleful effects of increased specialisation in humanities research and what is taken to be a related retreat from broader public conversation.[69] That is not the concern of this book, save to observe that the institutional trends I have noted must necessarily tend towards at least one and possibly two related but distinct developments: diversification and specialisation. In history, for instance, the twentieth century has seen a gradual widening of the perspectives from which history can be written, to take in first the social and the economic, and subsequently almost every conceivable angle of view.[70] (I have already noted the difference in character of the *Oxford History of the British Empire* when compared to its predecessor.)

The point is moot, however, as to whether such diversification necessarily entails specialisation, when defined as the confinement of *all* one's work to one area and a reluctance or inability to range more widely. Be that as it may, the academic publishing industry has certainly provided ever more specialised options for work in each smaller and smaller niche. Already in the 1960s, scholars were noting the proliferation of new specialist journals

---

[68] J. B. Thompson, *Books in the Digital Age: The Transformation of Academic and Higher Education Publishing in Britain and the United States* (Polity Press, 2005), pp. 93–4.

[69] S. Collini, *Absent Minds: Intellectuals in Britain* (Oxford University Press, 2006), pp. 451–71; I. Tyrrell, *Historians in Public: The Practice of American History, 1890–1970* (University of Chicago Press, 2005), pp. 25–40.

[70] Bentley, *Modernizing England's past*, pp. 120–40, 223–5; J. Kenyon, *The History Men* (2nd edition, Weidenfeld and Nicolson, 1993), pp. 289–98.

across the disciplines; by the 1980s, it was a matter of relatively casual notice, and the trend has continued since.[71] Although it is hard to prove the point, it seems clear that edited collections, or at least some of them, have similarly ploughed deeper and narrower furrows. In the case of Benjamin Britten, a long-running Boydell and Brewer series contains recent edited volumes dealing with matters as diverse as Britten's textual choices, the international dimension of his music (both as a composer and in terms of reception), and on the relation between composer and community.[72]

In any one country, there are natural limits to diversification, since each sub-community of scholars must be of a certain size to be viable. Technological change has fundamentally altered this particular calculus. The development of the international conference in the 1970s and 1980s (a product of inexpensive air travel) was instrumental in the growth of collaboration between scholars in different countries. Internet-enabled global communication necessarily made the formation of distributed communities of scholars of more and more specialist areas easier again. Where specialisation is on grounds of subject rather than locality, a niche journal available online can serve a small but worldwide community. The open access (OA) *Journal of Buddhist Ethics*, for instance, celebrated its twentieth year in 2013.[73] Global communication by means of email, video conferencing and online document management has also made international

---

[71] P. O. Larsen and M. von Ins, 'The rate of growth in scientific publication and the decline in coverage provided by Science Citation Index', *Scientometrics* 84 (3), 2010, 575–603, noting the work of Derek J. de Solla Price in 1961; S. Collini, 'Against Prodspeak: "Research" in the Humanities', in Collini, *English Pasts: Essays in History and Culture* (Oxford University Press, 1999), p. 234; Jordanova, *History in Practice*, pp. 20–2.

[72] K. Kennedy (ed.), *Literary Britten: Words and Music in Benjamin Britten's Vocal Works* (Boydell and Brewer, 2018); L. Walker (ed.), *Benjamin Britten: New Perspectives on his Life and Work* (Boydell and Brewer, 2009); P. Wiegold and G. Kenyon (eds), *Beyond Britten: The Composer and the Community* (Boydell and Brewer, 2015).

[73] D. Keown and C. Prebish, 'Celebrating twenty years of the *Journal of Buddhist Ethics*', *Journal of Buddhist Ethics* 20, 2013, 37–9, at http://blogs.dickinson.edu /buddhistethics.

collaboration no more laborious to administer than very local projects; both production and distribution have been fundamentally affected. *Lux Mundi* was an Oxford book, *Soundings* a Cambridge one, and some collections still grow out of local soils. But the edited collection has also become a global format. The recent *Sage Handbook of Web History* contains work by forty-six contributors from almost every continent, and went from initial planning to publication in a little over three years.

2.6 The Edited Collection and the Formation of New Disciplines

Since the creation of distributed communities of work has become easier, the edited collection has increasingly been a means of both defining a field and creating a community. Two examples will suffice, one relatively slow-moving and the second rather more rapid in its development. In the case of Anglican studies, the 1988 volume *The Study of Anglicanism* predates the expansion to which I have referred.[74] Although it noted the rapid growing to independence (at least in institutional terms) of Anglican churches in the world outside the UK and North America in the previous four decades, the volume was confined to established issues that would have concerned the readers of *Soundings*: history, theology and the practice of worship. All but one of the thirty-one contributors were from the British Isles or North America; all but three were clergy; all but two were male.

Since then, the notion of 'Anglican studies' has gradually emerged with the wider recognition, under the influence of a postcolonial turn in the academy, that the field involved more than simply the study of the Church of England in its place at the centre of a family of offspring churches formed under conditions of empire. The *Journal of Anglican Studies* was founded in 2003, but the *Oxford Handbook of Anglican Studies* (2016)[75] illustrated the shift in the field. With scholars from almost every continent – with a greater proportion of women and those who were not ordained ministers – the

---

[74] S. Sykes and J. Booty (eds), *The Study of Anglicanism* (Society for Promoting Christian Knowledge, 1988).

[75] M. Chapman, S. Clarke and M. Percy (eds), *The Oxford Handbook of Anglican Studies* (Oxford University Press, 2015).

approaches employed were historical and theological, but also now embraced aesthetics, demography, law and sociology. Its approach is kaleidoscopic rather than systematic, which reflects both the new fluidity of the idea of 'Anglicanism', and the range of perspectives which needed to be taken into account.

A second, more recent example is from what was an entirely new field of historical inquiry: that of Web history. The field was doubly new for historians; opinions have differed as to whether to place the inception of 'Anglicanism' in the sixteenth century or at some other point, but the World Wide Web itself is not yet three decades old. Not only is Web history a field of very contemporary history into which scholars often fear to venture. It also presents formidable new challenges of method, since its fundamental source material – the archived Web – represents an entirely new object of enquiry, for which the rules of interpretation are yet to settle themselves. Indeed, the process of Web archiving (in which field another edited collection, the 2006 volume *Web Archiving*,[76] was also highly influential) is itself in a state of constant flux, with consequent effects for the scholars wishing to use it.

Social scientists and other scholars of contemporary life were quick to see the Web as an object of study, but the business of thinking about the Web historically was slower to emerge, and when it did, it was a global movement that crossed many disciplines. It has been the province of historians of technology, and of the Internet in particular (which has a longer history). As well as that, scholars interested in every facet of life that manifested itself online have their own interests in the field. Much of the early work in each of these fields appeared in edited collections, the first of which was published in 2010. *Web History* was the result of a ground-breaking conference in Denmark in 2008, and contained essays on the scope and method of the field, along with case studies on particular questions: extremist nationalism; the aesthetics of Web advertising; webcam culture; the memorialisation of a mass shooting.[77] The same editor was partially responsible for another volume of essays on national broadcasters, among

---

[76] J. Masanès (ed.), *Web Archiving* (Springer, 2006).

[77] N. Brügger (ed.), *Web History* (Peter Lang, 2010).

the first organisations to adopt the Web.[78] Subsequent collections of individual case studies have continued to appear (*The Web as History* (2017); *Web 25: Histories from the First 25 Years of the World Wide Web* (2017)), along with the first consideration of the notion of the national Web in 2019.[79] It was not until 2017 that the first specialist journal, *Internet Histories*, was founded, followed in 2018 by the *Sage Handbook of Web History*.[80] Only in the same year, 2018, was the first major monograph treatment of the field as a whole published, by Niels Brügger, editor of several of the volumes already mentioned.[81] The edited collection, then, provided a space in which a global discipline could form, at a time when neither a specialist journal nor a handbook could have been feasible. Essays that were by their very nature exploratory in terms of method and of source material, and that as such might have been rejected one by one by existing journals solely for their novelty, were able to find a venue all together.

2.7 Conclusion

To be sure, many edited volumes have a heterogenous character. The fresh writing-up of new primary research, the synthesis and assessment of the state of scholarship on a particular question, and directly polemical writing: all of these often co-exist in the same volumes and indeed in the same chapters. Some apparently very general work has been issued by publishers traditionally regarded as academic, and highly influential primary research by publishers not commonly regarded as academic. However, that is simply to show the porousness, not to say artificiality, of the division of scholarly

---

[78] M. Burns and N. Brügger (eds), *Histories of Public Service Broadcasters on the Web* (Peter Lang, 2012).

[79] N. Brügger and R. Schroeder (eds), *The Web as History* (University College London Press, 2017); N. Brügger (ed.), *Web 25: Histories from the First 25 Years of the World Wide Web* (Peter Lang, 2017); N. Brügger and D. Laursen (eds), *The Historical Web and Digital Humanities: The Case of National Web Domains* (Routledge, 2019).

[80] N. Brügger and I. Milligan (eds), *The SAGE Handbook of Web History* (SAGE, 2018).

[81] N. Brügger, *The Archived Web* (MIT Press, 2018).

writing in the humanities between 'research', 'scholarship' and more publicly orientated work, as is sometimes attempted.

The case studies I have laid out show a rich interplay in edited volumes, as scholars have been brought together to add to and to assess the state of an issue, or the current state – indeed, the whole purpose – of a discipline. As well as assessing the present, they have also looked to the future. In some cases that conversation has been confined within the academy, sometimes with those outside listening in. Sometimes scholars in universities have addressed issues of contemporary importance in partnership with those outside with particular stakes in those matters. Sometimes these volumes have been the natural outgrowth of an existing group of scholars; at other times, they have been assembled by an editor or a publisher, sometimes including scholars with opposing views. What emerges overall, however, is a profoundly *communal* and *conversational* endeavour, examples of which may be multiplied across many of the particular sub-disciplines with which readers will themselves be familiar.

My point is not to suggest that precisely these kinds of configurations of individuals, subject and context are to be found in all those sub-disciplines, or that this culture of collective working is as strong in each field. We should, however, endeavour to understand both the history and the diversity of current working practices across all the disciplines before accepting at face value the edited collection meme complex. I shall return to the idea of the scholarly community in the conclusion.

3 The Present

What of the present state of the edited collection? In the Introduction I characterised current perceptions of edited collections as memes in a particular meme complex: simple, memorable and conducive to action. This section examines each of the memes in detail, and explores how far the perception can be grounded in empirical observation. The several memes concern the inadequacy of peer review, a supposed lack of both visibility and accessibility, and a citation deficit in comparison with journal articles. I also examine the importance of systems of research assessment, particularly in the UK. However, I begin with the publishing industry, and the perception that it has been in flight from the edited collection as a format.

3.1 Authors and Publishers

Since their commissioning decisions are unsurprisingly not open to scrutiny, it is difficult to document the enthusiasm of academic publishers for the edited collection. However, the idea that publishers have been in retreat from the format has taken root among authors and editors. In 2013, one commissioning editor (in politics and international relations) reported being approached by prospective editors 'in guilty tones', as if the game were already up for the edited collection.[82] A 2017 report on the academic book in the UK stated as a fact that although the edited collection was still valued by scholars, it was 'falling out of favour' with publishers.[83] Some of the scholars interviewed (of sufficient experience to have the necessary length of perspective) had the similar impression that it had become harder in recent years to persuade a publisher to accept an edited collection. One theologian had understood from a friend in the industry that one major publisher had instructed commissioning editors not to entertain the format at all; the same press was also named by another interviewee (a historian) as having largely withdrawn from the format.

The perception is not universal, however, as some survey responses indicated a belief that, far from it becoming more difficult, there was in fact now a proliferation of such volumes. The question could be settled by a detailed analysis of each publisher's catalogues over time, which has not been attempted for this study. However, that the crisis is overstated can be

---

[82] The press in question was Rowman and Littlefield. The statement was made in August 2013: A. Reeve, 'Making edited collections work', *Rowman & Littlefield* (22 August 2013), retrieved 17 December 2019 from https://web.archive.org /web/20160306223845/http://www.rowmaninternational.com/comment/mak ing-edited-collections-work-a-publishers-perspective.

[83] M. Deegan, *Academic Book of the Future Project Report* (The Academic Book of the Future), p. 32, retrieved 10 February 2019 from https://academicbookfuture .org/end-of-project-reports-2/.

seen in the Bibliography of British and Irish History (BBIH), where (although the total number of publications has risen) the relative proportions of monographs, articles and chapters remained all but unchanged between 1996 and 2015. However, it does seem that, even if the overall number of edited collections has remained steady, there has been a redistribution of market share among publishers, with some presses taking a strategic decision to specialise. The survey returned data about some 281 edited volumes completed or begun in the last ten years (across the humanities), from no fewer than 91 individual presses, but very prominent in the data was Routledge (including titles taken on under the acquisition of Ashgate), with some forty-four volumes, 16 per cent of those reported. Similarly, a recent analysis of the 2014 Research Excellence Framework (REF) in the UK from the British Academy found that, although the number of publishers that issued at least some collections was very large, fully two-thirds of the chapters submitted were in volumes published by a group of only thirty publishers; for the arts and humanities, a group of eight publishers accounted for more than half.[84] It is not quite clear, then, that there has been a general 'falling out of love' with the genre (the phrase of one interviewee) but a repositioning of the players in the market.

However, even if there has not been a general denigration of the format, there is some evidence of a more taxing requirement from commissioning editors to make the case for the rationale for a volume before acceptance. This is consistent with a broader trend for monographs, in which publishers have come to pay much greater attention to the likely sales for a volume, as the general expected sales have fallen.[85] One series editor interviewed also thought that the bar had been raised higher for edited collections than for monographs in his series; one publisher (interviewed by the British Academy) spoke of a 'guilty until proven innocent' approach to decision-making.[86] More than one publisher has published guidance for prospective editors. Much of this advice is about the practicalities of the process after acceptance, but all of it in various ways stresses the need for a clear sense of

---

[84] *Open Access and Book Chapters*, pp. 6, 32.
[85] Thompson, *Books in the Digital Age*, pp. 134–7.
[86] *Open Access and Book Chapters*, p. 28.

why the volume is necessary, and what it will achieve.[87] In general, it is hard to see why this should be anything other than welcome; I shall return shortly to the role of the editor in articulating that sense.

3.2 The Question of Quality

Arguably the single feature that has most clearly distinguished scholarly writing from other forms of publication is its subjection to the judgement of peers before it is published. Of course, there is a great deal of published writing that is original, incisive and important that does not undergo any form of review by other scholars. However, if for no other reason than to limit the volume of work which scholars know they must read, some sort of filtering has usually been applied. Although it was not inevitably so, one particular form of peer review has come to be regarded as the ideal: double-blind review (where neither reviewer nor reviewed know the identity of the other), classically brokered by the editorial staff of a journal. Double-blind review has taken on something of a totemic status in discussions about scholarly publishing, even if in fact its hold varies between disciplines.

More than one scholar has noted the remarkably recent solidification of this particular 'gold standard'. Before the 1950s, review was more often in the hands of journal editors and the standing committees they convened. Only gradually did the practice spread, particularly during the 1970s, only becoming the norm in the 1990s, even among journals now regarded as having a high status.[88] Significant doubt has also been cast on the degree to which anonymity is desirable in theory or uniformly achievable in practice,

---

[87] Reeve, 'Making edited collections work'; Palgrave Macmillan, 'Editing an essay collection', *Palgrave Macmillan*, retrieved 25 March 2019 from www.palgrave.com/br/palgrave/book-authors/your-career/mid-career-scholars-hub/editing-an-essay-collection/7487710; E. Brennan, 'Framing and proposing an edited volume for publication', *Manchester University Press* (17 February 2016), retrieved 25 March 2019 from www.manchesteruniversitypress.co.uk/articles/framing-and-proposing-an-edited-volume-for-publication/.

[88] N. Moxham and A. Fyfe, 'The Royal Society and the prehistory of peer review, 1665–1965, *Historical Journal* 61 (4), 2018, 863–89, at 887–8; M. Goldie, 'Fifty years of the *Historical Journal*', *Historical Journal* 51 (4), 2008, 821–55, at p. 839.

a point with particular force in smaller fields such as predominate in the humanities.[89] Anecdotal evidence also abounds for the abuse of power by unscrupulous reviewers; more fundamentally, others have cast doubt on whether it in fact achieves at all what it is designed to achieve.[90] But faith in the system remains widespread nonetheless. Despite significant experimentation both with non-anonymised prepublication peer review, and also with post-publication review by readers online, it remains largely accepted as the standard. As one insider noted, this is because there is thought to be no obvious scalable alternative, but also simply because both scholars and editors believe that it works, despite its demonstrable flaws: 'how odd', he noted, 'that science should be rooted in belief'.[91]

A component part of the meme complex of the edited collection is a similar belief that the peer review applied is less robust than that for journals. (It is a curious feature of the debate that, while the same doubt is sometimes expressed about the peer review for monographs, where procedures are largely the same, the high esteem in which the format is held seems unaffected.)[92] Although based not on any systematic studies of actual practice, this particular belief has been well established in the written commentary for some years. Although it is sometimes expressed in terms of the general difficulty or otherwise of having work accepted for publication in one format against another, it amounts to the same.[93] One of the

---

[89] D. Pontille and D. Torny, 'The blind shall see! The question of anonymity in journal peer review', *Ada. A journal of Gender, New Media and Technology* 4, retrieved 26 March 2019 from https://adanewmedia.org/2014/04/issue4-pontilletorny/. One study found that reviewers were able to guess correctly the identity of at least one author of papers submitted to three international software engineering conferences for between one in ten and one in four papers: C. Le Goues, Y. Brun, S. Apel et al., 'Effectiveness of anonymization in double-blind review', *Communications of the ACM* 61 (6), 2018, 30–3.

[90] R. Smith, 'Peer review: a flawed process at the heart of science and journals', *Journal of the Royal Society of Medicine* 99 (4), 2006, 178–82.

[91] Smith, 'Peer review', p. 182.

[92] See, for instance, Crossick, *Monographs*, juxtaposing p. 27 with pp. 17–20.

[93] A large-scale survey, conducted in 2014 by the OAPEN Project, of UK scholars in the humanities and social sciences found that, across all career stages, scholars

most substantial contributions to the debate, published in 2005, noted that the assumption was already widespread in the USA but (from the author's own experience as an editor in medieval history) argued that publishers, sensitised to the criticism, had already begun to place greater emphasis on quality control.[94] Yet the perception has persisted, in blog posts and career advice columns, and in official reports. A professor of law told the British Academy in 2019 that 'as mentors, we always advise younger colleagues to avoid publishing too much in edited collections, and to go for peer-reviewed journal articles. Edited collections can be absolutely excellent, but there is a rigour to a peer-reviewed journal process that might not be there in an edited collection: *it's not double-blind peer review*' (my italics).[95] Some commentators have suggested that the issue was not universal, but only a marker of the worst cases;[96] others accepted the idea almost as a maxim about the format as a whole.[97] In response, some publishers entered the fray to stress the robustness of their processes.[98]

believed it considerably less difficult to have their work published as a book chapter than as a journal article. Although the research did not investigate what those perceived difficulties were, the perception is clear. 'Researcher survey, 2014: report', *OapenUK*, pp. 8–9, retrieved 30 September 2019 from http://oapen-uk.jiscebooks.org/research-findings/researcher-survey-2014/.

[94] C. J. Nederman, 'Herding cats: the view from the volume and series editor', *Journal of Scholarly Publishing* 36 (4), 2005, 221–8, at pp. 222–3.

[95] *Open Access and Book Chapters*, p. 28.

[96] J. Weiler, 'On my way out – advice to younger scholars III: edited book', *Blog of the European Journal of International Law* (5 October 2016), retrieved 1 March 2019 from www.ejiltalk.org/on-my-way-out-advice-to-young-scholars-iii-edited-book/; F. Rojas, 'Let's talk about edited collections', *orgtheory.net* (28 July 2011), retrieved 1 March 2019 from https://orgtheory.wordpress.com/2011/07/28/lets-talk-about-edited-volumes/.

[97] A. Chapnick and C. Kukuchka, 'The pros and cons of editing a collection of essays', *University Affairs* (10 May 2016), retrieved 1 March 2016 from www.universityaffairs.ca/career-advice/the-scholarly-edition/the-pros-and-cons-of-editing-a-collection-of-essays/.

[98] T. Clague, 'Unbundling is over-rated: on the value of contributing to an edited book', *LSE Impact Blog* (5 March 2015), retrieved 1 February 2019 from http://

The perception was also clearly visible in the survey questionnaire results. Respondents were asked: 'In general, would you say that the peer review processes for edited collections, in comparison to journals, are more effective, less effective or about as effective?' Some 37 per cent of those who responded thought the processes were less effective. After those who had recorded an answer of 'Don't know' were disregarded, this figure climbed to 44 per cent. The figures were very similar among those who had not themselves published any of their work in an edited collection in the last ten years, and so were most reliant on the perceptions of others. It would seem that familiarity with edited collections tended slightly to increase confidence in the process. Even then, among the fifty respondents who had published most often in edited collections, still 40 per cent thought the processes in general less effective, while only 12 per cent thought them more effective.

Opinions among interviewees also varied, based on their own experience. One historian, and former head of department in a Russell Group university, recalled his work going through fewer iterations in collections than with journals; another (also a historian, from outside the UK) felt that the reviews received from journal reviewers had a more critical edge, a greater element of challenge. However, others had the opposite impression, that the feedback from collection editors in particular was in fact more engaged and exacting than a paragraph or two from a distracted journal reviewer. One suggested that editors did more than journals to draw out the potential in a draft that still needed work; several editors reported having themselves taken on the task of substantially rewriting large parts of some chapters, usually without any credit. The same editors were largely willing, and had been prepared in the past, to cut chapters from a volume if they were received too late (or not at all) or were too weak to include, even after several drafts, and even at the cost of a volume missing a chapter on an important topic if no replacement could be found. The presence of a substandard chapter goes to the reputation of the editor to a degree, and so (s)he has an incentive that a journal reviewer does not.

blogs.lse.ac.uk/impactofsocialsciences/2015/03/05/unbundling-is-over-rated-value-edited-books/.

At least part of the perception is likely to be due to the relative lack of transparency about the procedures employed. While many, indeed perhaps most, journals make clear their peer-review policy, the reader with an edited collection in hand has only a preface or introduction with which to judge, and these vary in what they disclose about the process. In these circumstances, to assume the lowest standard of review in the absence of information to the contrary is a rational precaution. One response from the publishing industry is the recent Guaranteed Peer Reviewed Content labelling system in Belgium, a voluntary scheme which requires publishers to provide evidence of at least two external reports on a book that is certified.[99] The symbol is printed on the book's colophon.

What of current practice? Both interviews and survey point to a wide variety of peer-review practices for edited collections. Respondents to the questionnaire were asked: 'How was [the volume in which your work appeared] peer reviewed?'[100] Nearly 60 per cent reported that their volume had undergone review by at least one external reader. Only a very small number reported that the editor of a book series had reviewed the manuscript. Nearly 10 per cent had been reviewed by the other contributors. Practice also varied among volumes with the same publisher; none of the publishers for whom more than a handful of volumes appeared in the data had anything like a settled policy on external review, to judge from the recollection of their contributors. Although the picture is mixed, the data cannot be made to support a general supposition that edited volumes are not peer reviewed; to that extent, the meme is mistaken.

[99] www.gprc.be/en/, retrieved 21 March 2019.

[100] While some of the responses were from editors, the majority were from contributors. It is at least conceivable therefore that (i) the total of 274 includes some duplication (if more than one contributor to a volume responded to the survey); (ii) that contributors were not aware of peer review undertaken earlier in the process; and (iii) that if chapters were sent to external review, that that fact was not revealed, but the comments provided in some digested form by the editors. As a result, if (iii) was indeed the case, the proportion of volumes subject to external review may be an underestimate.

One form of peer review which is sometimes employed, but is not yet common, is a formalised mutual review of chapters by the other contributors to the volume. I myself have now experienced such a process a number of times. In each case I have known the identity of the author whose work I reviewed (since I had seen the volume proposal), but did not know by whom my own chapter was reviewed. If the editor(s) have assembled the right group of contributors, it is highly likely to include precisely the people to whom a journal editor would have turned to conduct the review; they are, in fact, peers. (Indeed, in some cases there may be some difficulty in finding competent external reviewers who are not ineligible by dint of being a contributor to the volume themselves.) While the process adds additional time to what can already be a protracted process, it arguably aligns the interests of the reviewer with those of the volume as a whole more clearly than in a journal context. While undertaking a review for a journal, the reviewer has no particular incentive to engage with the task diligently and constructively, save for his or her intrinsic commitment to the abstract ideal of the system. In an edited collection, the reviewer stands to gain directly from their own chapter appearing in the strongest possible company, and so has an incentive to provide the most constructive feedback. For the same reason, they also stand to lose if complicit in allowing an irretrievably flawed chapter to be published alongside their own work. Although by no means common, such a system deserves serious consideration by both editors and publishers, as an addition to rather than as a substitute for third-party review.

Such certification schemes as the Belgian one, although constructive, are nonetheless predicated on the transplantation of the journal model of peer review into a book economy. The review economy in the case of books has perforce been different to that for journals, with greater reliance placed on the role of series and commissioning editors, and at the proposal rather than draft stage. This makes explicit the fact that peer review has in fact two elements. A filtering for quality – for the basic soundness of the execution of the work – is perforce only possible once a work is written; the assessment of significance – a judgement of which research is most important – need not happen at the same time. In the case of the edited collection, that function is moved to an earlier stage in the process, rather than after it has ended. The task of deciding which areas are in need of fresh attention is in the hands of the editor(s) of the volume itself, as they create a proposal for a publisher. With that idea in mind, they must decide which individual pieces of work together meet the brief, by inviting contributors, listening to papers in conference or sifting through abstracts. Then must the editor of a series (if there is one) be convinced of the intellectual worth of the project; the commissioning editor of the press concerned must then be persuaded both of the scholarly importance and that the market is such that sufficient sales are likely. Then that proposal is often itself subject to external review. One interviewee (an editor) had seen their proposal for a new handbook volume sent to four external readers; the proposal for another volume in which work of my own is to appear was reviewed by no fewer than seven readers. Only once a book is in draft does the second part of the process – the screening for soundness of execution – begin.

Ultimately, however, much rests in the hands of the editors. It is up to them to arrange a form of quality control appropriate to the volume and to the contributors, and it is to their reputation that a substandard volume would go. I shall have more to say about the issue of trust in the final section, but the survey results were revealing in this regard. In the case of the volumes that had only been reviewed by the editor(s), respondents had two options: to answer either 'by the editors' or 'it was not peer reviewed'. Only a very small proportion of respondents chose the latter option, which indicates that scholars by and large regard editors as peers for this purpose. Were there a strong attachment to the idea of external review as the only acceptable form, the proportion would surely have been larger. In sum, the lionisation of one particular form of peer review is misapplied in the context of the edited collection. Although the practice is different, it is far from clear that it is inferior; once again, the meme is probably incorrect.

3.3 The Role of the Editor

If in need of a refreshed perspective on their own woes, our fictitious editors Robin and Lucy needed to look no further than the experience of the *Cambridge Medieval History*. At one stage, the project had no definitive list of the contributions under contract, or postal addresses for the authors; at a different time, the subeditor could not communicate with the editor as she had no postal address for him. After years of delays, some contributors had assumed that the History was no longer a going concern; others produced work on time only to be told that the editors had no record of having commissioned it.[101] The History is perhaps an extreme case, but the kind of mistakes of project management that Robin and Lucy made in their ill-fated volume are not uncommon. They are, however, also eminently avoidable, and there is significant published advice on the matter, on which I shall not elaborate in detail.[102] In general, the editor needs to set a realistic schedule at the outset, and be able both to depart from it when necessary but also enforce it at other times. Communication must be clear, such that contributors know precisely to what it is they are contributing, in what form and by which time. Whichever process of review there is, its shape needs to be clear to the contributors, as must be the understanding that it is to be taken with the utmost seriousness. As already mentioned, editors need also the courage to be firm with the recalcitrant, and (if necessary) to take difficult decisions to exclude chapters that either are inadequate or arrive too late. Many editors reported the benefits of sharing the editorship with another, for mutual support, and division of the workload; teams of editors, some senior and some junior, are often able between them to deal with

---

[101] Linehan, 'Cambridge Medieval History', *passim*.

[102] L. Edwards, 'Editing academic books in the humanities and social sciences: maximising impact for effort', *Journal of Scholarly Publishing* 44 (1), 2012), 61–74, at pp. 64–70; A. Pohl, 'Sammelband herausgeben: gelernt', *Übertext* (3 June 2014), retrieved 22 April 2019 from www.uebertext.org/2014/03/; A. Chapnick and C. Kukuchka, 'Choosing the right contributors' *University Affairs* (13 July 2016), retrieved 22 April 2019 from www.universityaffairs.ca /career-advice/the-scholarly-edition/choosing-right-contributors/;

P. Thomson, 'Two big hassles in editing and what you can do about them', *Patter* (9 September 2013), retrieved 22 April 2019 from https://patthomson.net /2013/12/09/two-big-hassles-in-editing-a-book-and-what-you-can-do-about -them/; M. Carrigan, 'Some reflections on editing books and special issues while doing a Ph.D.', *Mark Carrigan* (17 June 2013), retrieved 20 March 2019 from https://markcarrigan.net/2013/06/17/some-reflections-on-editing-books- and-collections-while-doing-a-phd/.

difficulties with recalcitrant contributors, where relationships might otherwise become strained.

Perhaps above all, editors themselves need to take seriously the size of the task, and the amount of time that it will require. Lord Acton had taken on the shaping of the *Cambridge Modern History* at the age of 62, and the work was the principal burden of his last years. One historian noted that he wrote almost nothing else himself at the time, and nothing at all for the History itself; another thought the work had killed him.[103] Several of those interviewed, although having survived to tell the tale, testified to the costliness of the task.

Why, then, should anyone take on such an assignment? Opinions varied among interviewees as to the balance of intrinsic and extrinsic motivation. One historian in mid-career, who had not been an editor, wondered whether to edit a collection was an unspoken expectation of someone at his stage of career; another, more junior scholar (also a historian) had recently taken on an editorship after worrying for some time that not to have done so had made it more difficult to secure an academic job. At the same time, it was not clear to what degree the work of the editor was valued by others, and there was also a sense that it might be safer for one's career to spend the time on a monograph instead. (I shall return to the question of research assessment in the UK shortly.)

Several others articulated their motivation in rather more positive terms, as an obligation to a discipline rather than to an employer or for the good of one's career. Others talked of rewards that balanced the costs: of the opportunity to shape a field where one had neither the time nor the expertise to write a monograph on the same subject. Others again talked of the inherent reward of helping to build new communities of scholars, or to strengthen existing ones. And it is on the strength of the editor's vision that perhaps the success of even the most well-managed edited collection most clearly depends. To borrow a musical metaphor from one interviewee, the editor must be a composer and not merely a concert promoter; the task is not merely the bringing together of a group of soloists to perform one after another in one venue, but the

---

[103] Clark, 'Cambridge Modern History', p. 63; Kenyon, *The History Men*, p. 145.

selection and then guidance of those voices such that what emerges is an ensemble performance. To extend the metaphor, the performance will certainly be polyphonic, and indeed on occasion may be dissonant, but it must nonetheless be recognisable as one emerging from a single intelligence.

The question may be asked, and has been asked: is there too much power in the hands of the editor? Is the face-to-face nature of the process, where names are known, prone to the exercise of patronage and the cementing of existing networks at the expense of those outside? It is hard to exclude the possibility entirely, but the impression of those interviewed was the opposite, in fact. As contributors, most had been approached by editors whom they had not previously known. Those who had been editors had not composed a whole volume from only their closest associates, and this should not surprise us; the diversification and globalisation of scholarship in the last few years now makes volumes like *Soundings*, made up of the work of scholars from a single faculty, hard to imagine. One study on the situation in Flanders (in the humanities and social sciences) concluded that editors did not in general only include others from within their networks, and also that engagement with previously unknown scholars led to subsequent collaboration on other projects.[104] Although an editor is in a position of trust, it is not clear that that trust is often abused. I shall return to the issue of trust in the Conclusion.

3.4 Visibility and Access

A persistent metaphor in the various critiques of the edited collection is that of 'burying' one's work. In 2012, the Oxford University psychologist Dorothy Bishop published a widely cited blog post, based on an analysis of the citations of her own work, finding that book chapters were considerably less cited than journal articles. 'Quite simply,' she wrote, 'if you write a chapter for an edited book, you might as well write the paper and then

---

[104] T. Ossenblok, R. Guns and M. Thelwall, 'Book editors in the social sciences and humanities: an analysis of publication and collaboration patterns of established researchers in Flanders', *Learned Publishing* 28 (4), 2015, 261–73.

bury it in a hole in the ground.'[105] The wider argument is that, even supposing that a book chapter was of the highest quality and significance, scholars are less likely to be aware of its existence than if it had appeared in a journal, and that (once its existence was known) are less able to obtain a copy.[106] Of all the individual memes in the complex, it is this that most obviously has some weight. However, these two issues are far from insoluble, and the publishing and library sectors have already since 2012 done a certain amount to solve them.

Firstly, the question of visibility. It is clearly the case that the book chapter has tended to have a smaller 'metadata footprint', both online and in library catalogue systems. Journal articles have for some years been routinely supplied with abstracts and keyword information, whereas publishers have tended to list only authors and chapter titles on their own sites (and often not even that). To borrow a phrase, the 'article economy' has been stronger than the corresponding 'chapter economy'.[107] However, this issue is technologically straightforward to solve, and in very recent years some book publishers have begun to publish abstracts for individual chapters in edited collections and indeed in monographs, and to make that data

[105] D. Bishop, 'How to bury your academic writing', *BishopBlog* (26 August 2012), retrieved 1 February 2019 from http://deevybee.blogspot.com/2012/08/how-to-bury-your-academic-writing.html. From the responses, see (for instance), P. Thomson, 'Is writing a book chapter a waste of time?', *Patter* (27 August 2012), retrieved 1 September 2018 from https://patthomson.net/2012/08/27/is-writing-a-book-chapter-a-waste-of-time/; P. Webster, 'On the invisibility of edited collections', *Webstory* (14 January 2013), retrieved 1 October 2019 from https://peterwebster.me/2013/01/14/on-the-invisibility-of-edited-collections/.

[106] The 2014 UK research survey by the OAPEN Project showed that, in general, researchers were significantly more likely to perceive it as easy or very easy to access journal articles than book chapters: 'Researcher survey 2014: report', p. 10.

[107] K. Anderson, 'Bury your writing – why do academic book chapters fail to generate citations?', *The Scholarly Kitchen* (28 August 2012), retrieved 1 January 2019 from https://scholarlykitchen.sspnet.org/2012/08/28/bury-your-writing-why-do-academic-book-chapters-fail-to-generate-citations/

available to libraries for use in their catalogues.[108] Expenditure on e-books doubled in the four years to 2012/13 among university and national libraries in the UK,[109] and this provision of metadata is a natural accompaniment to the acquisition of an e-book edition as well as (or instead of) a print edition, although it is not yet the case that chapter-level metadata is supplied as standard. (Not all university libraries have in-house cataloguers and so must depend on what is supplied.) As and when libraries are also supplied with chapter-level metadata for volumes that have not yet been purchased (as part of a move towards patron-driven acquisition (PDA)), the visibility gap will be closed further.[110] An obvious complement to this is the assignment of individual digital object identifiers (DOIs) to each chapter, as is already the case with journal articles and indeed datasets and other resources. As and when these measures are adopted universally (and the additional cost to the publishers is negligible while the advantages are significant), this should largely remove this particular problem.

Away from library catalogues, there is surprisingly little known about the working habits of humanities scholars, and in particular about their methods of discovering new work that they should read. It is not at all clear whether scholars monitor the new issues of particular journals, certain publishers or subject bibliographies (where they exist), or rely on social media, email lists, word of mouth or indexing services such as Google Scholar, or combine some or all of these methods. That said, for those who do use citation indexes, both the monograph and the edited collection have been poorly served.[111] The Book Citation Index was created only as

---

[108] Jubb, *Academic Books*, p. 163.

[109] Crossick, *Monographs*, p. 23. The group under analysis was the members of the Society of College, National and University Libraries.

[110] On patron-driven acquisition in general, see the essays in David A. Swords (ed.), *Patron-Driven Acquisitions: History and Best Practices* (De Gruyter, 2011).

[111] The argument made by the British Academy: 'British Academy responds to Lord Stern's independent review of the Research Excellence Framework (REF)', *The British Academy* (4 April 2016), para 10, p. 5, retrieved 17 December 2019 from www.thebritishacademy.ac.uk/news/british-academy-responds-lord-sterns-independent-review-research-excellence-framework-ref. See also S. Tanner, *An Analysis of the Arts and Humanities Submitted Research*

recently as 2010 as part of the Web of Science, with the aim of indexing 10,000 books each year across all disciplines; in the same year, the BBIH alone recorded over 3,800 monographs and a further 718 edited collections.[112] The Google Scholar service (assuming for a moment that it will be maintained as a live service in the long term) has the potential to change the balance, as its coverage of those monographs and edited collections that have metadata available (or the full text in the Google Books service) is considerably wider.[113]

There must necessarily be a causal link between visibility and availability for book titles, and indeed for any kind of publication: if it is not known, it cannot be acquired. What then of the issue of availability in particular: can a scholar as easily obtain a copy of an edited collection as a comparable journal, once aware of its existence and its contents? Put simply, will their library have a copy, either printed or digital? The question is very hard to frame, since the purchasing patterns of each library are unique; it is also difficult to identify particular volumes that might be meaningfully compared with particular journals in order then to compare the library holdings of each. However, when the academic publishing environment is surveyed as a whole, it seems clear that the availability of edited collections in relation to journals has worsened in recent years. Even on its own, the persistent general rise in book prices (noted in Section 2) would inevitably have led to the reduction in the number of books purchased by any one library, unless its budget had expanded to keep pace (which by and large has not been the case). It is often the case that the

Outputs to the REF2014 with a Focus on Academic Books: An Academic Book of the Future Report (The Academic Book of the Future, 2016), pp. 35–7.

[112] B. Erb, 'Beyond WorldCat: accessing scholarly output in books and edited monographs', *The Charleston Advisor* 15(2), 2013, 62–6, at p. 65.

[113] Although it has been noted that, even if the coverage is wider, the data for each chapter tends to be less complete than that for articles and conference proceedings: D. Zeitlyn and M. Beardmore-Herd, 'Testing Google Scholar bibliographic data: estimating error rates for Google Scholar citation parsing', *First Monday* 23 (11), 2018, https://firstmonday.org/ojs/index.php/fm/article/view/8658/7607.

pricing of e-book substitutes is no lower, and is often rather higher than a print edition.[114] It is also well attested that the cost of journal subscriptions has risen faster than library purchasing budgets, leading to the current revolt in both Europe and North America against Elsevier and other large journal publishers; the first major battle in a wider war.[115] This has necessarily therefore restricted the funds available for the purchase of other formats, including the edited collection. In the UK, the share of library spending allocated to book acquisition fell from 40 to 32 per cent in the decade to 1999/2000.[116] Even though in the decade to 2014 UK university library spending on books had been largely level in cash terms, it was still under pressure from increases in journal prices.[117]

Among the librarians interviewed, there was agreement about the issue, but an admission that it was relatively difficult to cancel a journal subscription, particularly when it was part of a larger bundle of journals from a single publisher. Under these conditions, the decision to cancel a journal subscription in order to buy an individual monograph or edited collection is an administratively difficult one to make, which tends to skew purchasing patterns towards inertia, and against the volume. It is likely that the tendency of book publishers to group titles into series to encourage the placing of standing orders is a measure against this. However, purchasing patterns vary widely, and while some libraries operate using such standing orders, or by means of approval plans (by which they receive from an intermediary all books on a particular topic from multiple publishers, to

---

[114] The situation is complex, in that an e-book may sometimes be purchased on a licensing basis that allows multiple users, a situation more comparable to the acquisition of multiple print copies rather than a single one. A project of the American Academy of Arts and Sciences found the average list price to be twice that of comparable print titles in data for the period 2009–13: 'Trends in the price of academic titles in the humanities and other fields', *Humanities Indicators* (2015), retrieved 16 September 2019 from www.humanitiesindicators.org/content/indicatordoc.aspx?i=10965.

[115] Anon, 'Germans edge towards the brink in dispute with Elsevier', *Times Higher Education*, 7 December 2017, p. 14; 'French say "no deal" to Springer as journal fight spreads', *Times Higher Education*, 12 April 2018, p. 9.

[116] Thompson, *Books in the Digital Age*, p. 105. [117] Crossick, *Monographs*, p. 24.

accept or return), others are more reactive. The precise effect of the shift to PDA, in which libraries set out to acquire only those volumes that academic staff and students know they require, and thus request, is hard to document.[118] The growing availability of single chapters for purchase (enabled by the chapter-level metadata noted earlier) is also increasing, with effects that are similarly hard to determine.

The nature of the edited volume itself has both positive and negative effects on visibility. Several interviewees thought that the juxtaposition of chapters added an additional means of discovery, whereby a reader who came to a particular volume for a single chapter was made aware of the other chapters in a manner that has no precise analogy in a journal context. If the availability of single chapters for purchase without the whole volume begins to prevail as a mode of access, this effect will necessarily be weakened, unless specific design decisions are taken in library management systems to expose the context from which the single chapter is drawn. More than one interviewee also made the point that very few readers outside the universities are able to access journals, unless they have membership of a learned society and receive its journal as part of their membership (which applies in only a small proportion of cases). This applies to the general reader but also to professionals of all kinds outside the universities to whom scholars might have something to say. Whether or not those readers are more likely to read a chapter in such a volume than in a journal depends on both the price and the visibility of the volume to those readers. However, it is clear that much of the work examined in the case studies in Section 2 could have not had the same impact outside the universities had the individual papers been published separately in journals.

There was, however, a trade-off between visibility to specific audiences (through a specialist journal) and to wider (and in particular interdisciplinary) readerships. Here both the potential and limitations of the special issue of a journal as an alternative to the edited collection come into focus. Such

---

[118] K. S. Fischer, M. Wright, K. Clatanoff, H. Barton and E. Shreeves, 'Give 'em what they want: a one-year study of unmediated patron-driven acquisition of e-books', *College and Research Libraries* 73 (5), 2012, 469–92. That PDA is a growing feature in the UK is confirmed by Crossick, *Monographs*, p. 24.

special issues are most effective (in terms of immediate visibility) when a specialist journal exists, the scope of which comprehensively embraces the whole set of articles. As soon as the contributions begin to escape from the corral of the journal's accustomed scope, authors and editors alike face a trade-off between reaching one very specific group of readers and those in the discipline more widely, and beyond.

All of these considerations apply in an environment where readers (or libraries) pay for access to scholarly publications. The final element to consider is the ongoing transition to open access (OA), given renewed impetus in recent months with the adoption by several European funding bodies of 'Plan S'. The debate over the particularities of humanities publishing in relation to OA is now a long one, and the plan has generated no little opposition.[119] However the plan is implemented, much depends on whether the resulting environment is one in which books (which in this policy context includes the edited collection) are made as visible and as accessible as journals. One of the ten principles of the plan is that 'the above principles shall apply to all types of scholarly publications, but it is understood that the timeline to achieve OA for monographs and books may be longer than 1 January 2020'.[120] The length of this delay is not easy to foresee at the time of writing. That it may be considerable is evident in that both publishers and scholars are (in the UK, at least) rather less prepared for OA of any kind for book than they are for journals. If the possible business models for OA for monographs are less developed than for journals, the edited collection is further behind still. The British Academy found that of the thirty publishers that published more than two-thirds of edited collections in 2014, less than a third had clearly defined policies for OA for chapters. It also argued that there is a commensurate lack of awareness among scholars of their options, and recommended that action be taken to address that lack.[121]

---

[119] Anon, 'Plan S "could prove fatal" for learned societies', *Times Higher Education*, 25 October 2018, p. 13; 'Plan S: shock or solution?', *Times Higher Education*, 13 September 2018, p. 15.

[120] cOAlition S, '10 Principles', *Plan S* (2019), retrieved 1 April 2019 from www.coalition-s.org/10-principles/.

[121] *Open Access and Book Chapters*, p. 38.

However long the delay may turn out to be, for as long as chapters are generally less available on an OA basis than journal articles, they will be less accessible.

The British Academy examined several potential business models for OA to edited collections as a unit, which despite their difficulties would preserve the relatedness of the collection. It is likely that the alternative, a green OA by means of deposit of individual chapters in several separate institutional or subject repositories, while improving the visibility and accessibility of individual chapters, would at the same time shear them of their context in the volume as a whole; the boosting of a chapter economy to match the article economy, at the cost of the loss of a collection economy. If the correct metadata is both created and then used, the reassembling of a group of chapters from multiple repositories is by no means beyond achieving, but it is not (at the time of writing) a common use case in institutional repositories, and would require careful implementation, most likely at a global scale. That some publisher resistance to such reassembling is likely can be inferred from some of the current stated policies on green OA, which rule out entirely any 'linking, collection or aggregation' on the part of the depositor.[122]

3.5 Research Assessment Policy

One of the most striking features of the recent history of universities, and of universities in the UK in particular, is the changed terms of the tacit contract between the higher education sector and government. Stefan Collini has shown that the purpose of the university has never been as stable as is sometimes supposed, but in recent years governments have come to regard the direct economic impact of research as one of the primary criteria by which to judge a university's performance.[123] This in itself might not necessarily have led to the kind of systems of research assessment now implemented in several countries, had it not been coupled with broader

---

[122] *Open Access and Book Chapters*, p. 42.

[123] S. Collini, 'What's Happening to Universities? Historical and Comparative Perspectives', in S. Collini (ed.), *Speaking of Universities* (Verso, 2017), pp. 15–35.

changes in the methods and ethos of public-sector management. Accountability, which arguably was always exercised privately to a certain degree, became linked with 'transparency', defined in a particular way as the visibility of those deliberations to the public gaze. It also became linked, when it need not necessarily have been so linked, with a certain cult of quantification and metric measures. The historian Jerry Z. Muller has coined the term 'metric fixation', a pervasive condition in public life with three symptoms: a faith in the supposed objectivity of numeric measures and the displacement of the professional judgement of experts; a belief that the making public of those metrics equates to accountability; and that better 'performance' is to be fostered by attaching reward and punishment – either financial or in terms of reputation – to the rankings that are the result.[124]

In some countries, the prejudice against the edited collection which I have described is built into systems of research assessment. In Norway, for instance, publications are counted rather than individually assessed, but such that chapters in edited collections score fewer points than accrue to journal articles. As Curt Rice, rector of Oslo Metropolitan University, observed, this is to declare a priori that the very best edited collection chapter is of a lower quality than the very worst published journal article: a patent absurdity.[125] Rice also observed, and an interview with a historian based in Norway confirmed, that scholars very quickly learned not to give their introductions to edited volumes the title 'introduction', since that would receive no points at all; a more perfect example of a systemic failure would be hard to find.

For authors in the UK, the point of contact has been with successive rounds of centralised national assessment of research: first the Research Assessment Exercise (RAE) which occurred in 2001 and 2008, and its

---

[124] J. Z. Muller, *The Tyranny of Metrics* (Princeton University Press, 2018), pp. 17–19.

[125] C. Rice, 'Three simple distinctions your government should eliminate from its research financing system', *Curt Rice* (7 November 2013), retrieved 30 January 2019 from http://curt-rice.com/2013/11/07/3-simple-distinctions-your-government-should-eliminate-from-its-research-financing-system/.

successor, the REF which was last carried out in 2014 and will be again in 2021. Although the RAE/REF has evolved with each iteration, it was and remains a means of attributing scores to individual pieces of published research based on their quality and significance and the ranking of academic departments (or 'units of assessment') based on the cumulative scores of their staff's work. On these rankings is the allocation of public funding then based, in part.

The RAE/REF has been criticised on several grounds, both going to the principle of such a system and to the particular faults and unintended consequences of each particular implementation.[126] In the case of edited collections, the criticism is slightly different to that in the Norwegian case. That said, it is in some senses more alarming since it speaks of a fundamental scholarly attitude – of the power of the meme – than of a fault of implementation with the particular system.

The guidance documentation for the 2008 RAE was, on the face of it, hospitable to the submission of edited collections, both as a whole (by the editor) and as individual chapters: the panel of assessors 'will be guided solely by its view of [the output's] research quality. All cited outputs will be judged on academic merit regardless of the medium ... or location of publication ... [the panels] will not treat any category of output as intrinsically superior or inferior to any other.'[127] Several interviewees recalled that in 2014 this had also been the advice from those subject specialist colleagues from other universities (often with experience on the assessment panels in previous years) brought in to advise on strategy. The documentation for the 2014 REF was similarly explicit that the exercise was agnostic as to publishing format, and the report for Main Panel D (dealing with the arts and humanities) made the point again after the exercise was completed, having

---

[126] D. Sayer, *Rank Hypocrisies: The Insult of the REF* (Sage, 2014).

[127] Research Assessment Exercise 2008, *Panel Criteria and Working Methods: Panel N* (2006), p. 24, retrieved 17 December 2019 from www.rae.ac.uk/pubs/2006/01/ . The point has been repeated in the guidance documentation for submissions to the forthcoming exercise in 2021: Research Assessment Exercise 2021, *Guidance on submissions* (2019), p. 50, retrieved 17 December 2019 from www.ref.ac.uk/publications/guidance-on-submissions-201901/.

clearly caught wind of the meme: 'quality of content, not type of output, dictated scores awarded', the sub-panel for History stated, 'and institutions that artificially selected by type of output may have thereby lowered their scores'.[128] However, the reality of university decision-making seems to have been just that.

So pervasive is the meme that the explicit guidance given has been widely discounted in the formation of individual university policies. Recollections of the 2008 exercise were that there was an informal yet very clear hierarchy of publication types, and that chapters, if submitted at all, should be few, and were certainly not to be the prime work in a portfolio:[129] to paraphrase one interviewee, there was clearly a game under way, of which the real rules were different to those in the rulebook. In 2014, at least one university went so far as to ban its staff from submitting collection chapters at all. Other interviewees, while not under such a ban, had been nonetheless strongly discouraged from putting chapters forwards, unless they could make a strong case for the merits of the individual piece of work. Even in those universities in which there was no specific guidance, interviewees still reported a need to make an individual case for an edited collection chapter, which was not necessary for a journal article.

Why there should be such a mismatch between the letter of public policy and its interpretation is hard to determine. It is at least possible that those administering universities without particular knowledge of the humanities tend to formulate policy in line with the working practices of the hard sciences, in which both book chapters and indeed monographs figure relatively little. (In 2014, 99.5 per cent of submissions to REF Main Panel A – which included medicine and biological sciences – were journal articles; the figure for chemistry, physics and maths was 94.4 per cent.)[130] A 2015 report on the monograph in the UK found some evidence of pressure within universities on humanities scholars to favour journals over even

---

[128] 'Unit of Assessment 30: History', in Research Excellence Framework 2014. *Overview Report by Main Panel D and Sub-panels 27 to 36*, p. 52.

[129] J. Carter Wood, 'Collections in crisis?', *Obscene Desserts* (25 February 2018), retrieved 24 April 2019 from http://obscenedesserts.eu/?p=36 .

[130] Tanner, *An Analysis of the Arts and Humanities*, p. 7.

monographs, a format similarly uncommon in the hard sciences.[131] Alternatively, concern has often been expressed as to the time pressure under which panel members have been required to work, assessing large bodies of work. Although the report of the 2014 REF took particular pains to reject the very idea, some of those interviewed imagined that a convenient rule of thumb based on publication format might have been a temptation to hard-pressed panel members, despite their best intentions.[132] Whatever the particular cause, universities have in some cases adopted policies based on an assessment of risk, in spite of the specified rules of the game. I shall return to the issue of risk in the conclusion.

But, despite the strength of the meme complex, and institutional pressure in at least some cases, edited chapters *were* submitted to the 2014 REF, and in large numbers, just over 9,000 in all. The profile varied significantly between disciplines: in philosophy, 2.6 journal articles were submitted for every chapter; in classics, in contrast, there were significantly more chapters than articles (the ratio being 0.8). Among the disciplines dealt with in Section 2, the ratios were 1.7 (history), 1.2 (theology and religious studies) and, for music (grouped together with drama, dance and the performing arts), 1.5. As well as individual chapters, editors also submitted whole edited volumes for assessment as a unit; one in five of the books submitted to Main Panel D was an edited volume.[133] The extent to which chapters were submitted solely because without them the scholar in question would have insufficient outputs to submit is very difficult to gauge (the required number was four). However, it is surely hard to imagine that all 9,000 chapters were submitted simply to make up the numbers. Whatever their

---

[131] Crossick, *Monographs*, pp. 18–19.

[132] There have consequently been calls for the effective anonymisation of the outputs as presented to panel members, both as to the identity of the author and the publication details: G. Farrell, 'For fairness, we need anonymous marking in the REF, too', *Times Higher Education* (11 January 2018), pp. 28–9. Cf. *Overview Report by Main Panel D and Sub-panels 27 to 36*, pp. 14, 52, 71, 76.

[133] Tanner, *An Analysis of the Arts and Humanities*, p. 7; for further analysis, see Crossick, *Monographs*, p. 14.

views are of the format as a whole, there seems to have been no shortage of scholars who regarded particular chapters as among their best work and were prepared to stake their reputation on declaring that view.

3.6 Citation

One recent historian of British universities first encountered the notion of judging the significance of academic work by the number of times it is cited by others in the late 1980s. His verdict was to the point: 'I didn't believe it when I first heard about it ... The idiocy involved in using this as an indicator of anything of importance in most fields is too obvious to need rehearsing.'[134] Thirty years on, it is far from clear that many humanities scholars would dissent very much from Stefan Collini's verdict. But since then, Jerry Zuller's metric fixation has achieved a remarkable cultural dominance, and (in the UK) dissatisfaction with the cost of the REF (mainly in terms of the time taken to individually assess each output) has led to an increased focus on metric methods of assessment. Although disputed for its own reasons, the prospect that peer assessment of work might in time be supplemented or even displaced by bibliometric assessment is far from remote.[135] As such, whether scholars accept the premise or not, the question of citation counting has become pressing. The final meme to be examined in this chapter is that which suggests that chapters are less likely to be cited.

The final question in the survey questionnaire attempted to uncover the underlying strength of this particular meme, once all of the other issues that I have examined were cleared away. It asked respondents to entertain a hypothetical situation in they have a piece of written work in hand, and have a choice where to place it. One option was a 'highly regarded journal, which you know (for the purposes of this question) will accept it'. The second option was 'an edited collection published by a major press,

---

[134] Collini, 'Against Prodspeak', p. 247.

[135] The literature on the broad area of bibliometrics is very large, but a sense of the overarching issues may be gained from J. Wilsdon, L. Allen, E. Belfiore et al., *The Metric Tide: Report of the Independent Review of the Role of Metrics in Research Assessment and Management* (Higher Education Funding Council for England, 2015).

edited by a highly respected scholar and containing the work of many prominent scholars [which] focusses on a significant research area'. The two would be held by a similar number of libraries; both would be available digitally and with an individual abstract for discovery purposes.

Given the choice, respondents were asked to indicate in which format their work would be most likely to be cited by others. A remarkable 62 per cent of those who responded thought that their work would be more cited if published in the journal; only 19 per cent thought the chapter would be more cited. The same piece of work, even when at its most visible both technologically and in terms of the company it keeps, would (in this view) make a lesser impact. For these scholars, then, the hold of the meme over the minds of their colleagues remains unshakeable. But does perception match reality; that is, are book chapters indeed cited less?

The proposition is in fact rather difficult to test, since it is perforce impossible to publish the same work in two ways and compare the results. There is no means of comparing particular volumes with particular journals, since the journal impact factor (which has itself been vigorously critiqued) has no equivalent in the book context.[136] As noted earlier, the major citation indices are too incomplete for the task. So, any attempt to identify the one hundred works cited most often and examine the proportions of articles in relation to chapters is likely to be meaningless. Instead, an alternative approach was adopted, testing a slightly different hypothesis. If edited collection chapters are indeed cited less in general, then we should expect to see a significant mismatch between the proportion of total publications that are chapters and the proportion of unique works cited that were chapters. Two datasets were chosen to address the hypothesis. First was the annual total publication numbers of works noticed by the BBIH; second was a newly compiled dataset of unique works cited in a random sample of articles on British and Irish history published in a selection of general historical journals.

---

[136] See, for instance, D. N. Arnold and K. K. Fowler, 'Nefarious numbers', *Notices of the American Mathematical Society* 58(3), 2011, 434–7. An earlier example is Per O. Seglen, 'Why the impact factor of journals should not be used for evaluating research', *British Medical Journal* 314 (1997), 498–502.

As noted earlier, the proportions of unique works by publishing format in the BBIH has remained stable in recent years (1996–2015). Excluding works in other formats, monographs have constituted between 26 and 28 per cent of the total, with 40–2 per cent being articles, with chapters forming the remaining 30–1 per cent. If articles and chapters are equally likely to be cited by others, we should therefore, broadly speaking, expect to see four articles being cited to every three chapters.

Forty articles on British and Irish history were selected at random from five prominent general historical journals, ten each from the years 2018, 2013, 2008 and 1998. Their subject coverage was not controlled, but their temporal coverage was, such that an even spread was ensured from the twelfth to the twentieth century. Between them, they cited 1,912 unique works, of which more than half (966) were monographs; a rather greater proportion than in the BBIH data. This should be no surprise, since monographs by definition are rather longer and thus there is more material to cite. More significant, however, is the ratio of articles to chapters. Some 493 journal articles were cited and 336 chapters, a ratio of 3 chapters to every 4.4 articles. This ratio is only slightly less than the 3:4 observed in the BBIH data, suggesting that there is not a clear citation deficit for chapters in relation to articles. Rough and ready though this comparison is, it should – in the absence of larger studies – at least lead one to question the strength of the perception revealed in the survey. Not only that; if the comments made already about the improving visibility of chapters are correct, then in theory we should expect to see the ratio change further in favour of chapters in the coming years.

4 Conclusion: The Future

How true to life, then, is the story of Robin and Lucy? In Section 3 I examined each of the main memes in the edited collection complex, and the degree to which they can be shown to be justified. While edited collection chapters have been less visible than journal articles, the problem is one of information systems rather than anything fundamental to the format; the situation has improved and is also likely to continue to improve, although much now depends on the implementation of mandatory OA. In spite of scholars' perceptions, it is not at all clear that there has been a generalised loss of confidence in the format among publishers. Without much further research, it is also hard to say (based on data for British and Irish history) that there is any universal citation deficit when chapters are compared with journal articles. I have also argued that although the systems of quality control commonly used for collections may be different to those for journals, it is not clear that they are any less robust. Much depends on the editor(s).

Despite the lack of empirical evidence, however, the meme complex remains strong, both in perceptions and in the way those perceptions are tacitly or openly embedded in systems of research assessment. There is a persistent misalignment between what scholars believe is in the best interest of their discipline (on the one hand) and their understandings of the professional incentives under which they must work. And such perceptions tend to be self-fulfilling, since a maligned publishing format will attract lesser work from scholars less committed to the task, and thus suffer in terms of quality, significance and impact. If this little Element has done anything to break that cycle, it will have achieved its aim.

The story of the edited collection in the last three decades is in part a story of the interplay of technological change, economics, public policy and the changing nature of the scholarly enterprise, where none is wholly cause or wholly effect. The advent, for instance, of the high price, small print run business model for printed books is surely both the product of technological change and changing demand in the market, and also both a response to and stimulant of increased specialisation. I would however argue that, had the edited collection not existed, it would have had to be invented in some other form, since it serves certain aspects of scholarly community at its best that are not served in other ways. There are, too, more fundamental factors of motivation and personality in play in the relation of individual and collective in academic life, which certainly pre-date the last few years, with which I now conclude.

4.1 Freedom and Community

The idea of academic freedom generally comes into view only when it is threatened in a direct way: by the compulsion of scholars, whether by governments or indeed their universities, to publish certain things and not others, in certain venues and not in others, and at a certain rate. To transpose Isaiah Berlin's famous distinction between two kinds of liberty out of its original context, the freedom from direction or constraint in this way is a form of negative liberty.[137]

The second of Berlin's two ideas is that of positive liberty: the freedom not so much from direct constraint as 'to be a subject, not an object; to be moved by reasons, by conscious purposes, which are my own, not by causes which affect me, as it were, from outside'.[138] In one of the critiques of the edited collection is a highly revealing phrase. To publish one's work in an edited collection, the author argued, is to allow oneself to be distracted by the thematic priorities of others: to divert time and effort into publishing work that, left to one's own devices, one might not have pursued. Instead, scholars – and particularly scholars early in their careers – should pursue instead their own 'sovereignly set research agenda'.[139] Positive academic liberty, in this sense, is the freedom to take sole control of one's work, to pursue one's fundamental intellectual purpose solely in accordance with its own logic.

In an earlier essay, Berlin made another distinction, between two kinds of intellectual personality: the hedgehog and the fox. The hedgehog knows one big thing whereas the fox knows something about many things; the hedgehog's instinct is to relate all things to a single, coherent vision; the fox's thought is centrifugal, operating on many levels, 'scattered or diffused'.[140] The scholarly hedgehog, then, is likely to value his or her academic sovereignty – or, his positive liberty – to a greater extent than does the fox; better to pursue one's singular vision than to be waylaid by contributing to a project conceived by others.

Berlin published both essays long before many of the pressures of publishing culture and academic assessment that I have detailed came to

---

[137] Berlin gave his inaugural lecture in Oxford in 1969, with the title 'Two concepts of liberty'. It is most easily found in I. Berlin, *Four essays on liberty* (Oxford University Press, 1969).

[138] Ibid., p. 131.   [139] Weiler, 'Advice to younger scholars'.

[140] I. Berlin, 'The Hedgehog and the Fox', in H. Hardy and A. Kelly (eds), *Russian Thinkers* (Penguin, 1994), pp. 22–3.

bear. However, although I have sought to remove a number of misconceptions concerning the edited collection, it may be that, for some scholars, the edited collection will always remain uncongenial for the constraints it must involve and for the distraction it may prove to be from their sovereign research agenda: an infringement of their positive academic liberty. They may wish to read no further, if they have indeed made it thus far. But there is in play a wider issue about the ideal nature of a scholarly community.

In Section 3, I argued that, far from being the reinforcer of the boundaries of existing scholarly cliques, the making of an edited collection often acts to widen those networks, and to create new ones. And there is another sense in which the state of the edited collection is an indication of the health of a certain idea of scholarly community, which persists still, although in inhospitable conditions. The fictional type is well established of the competitive academic, who will stop at nothing to achieve their ends, such as the grave-robbing Mortimer Cropper in A. S. Byatt's novel *Possession* (1990). It may be that the internalisation (in universities) of an imperative of competitiveness that Kathleen Fitzpatrick has outlined[141] – connected to a wider stress on the 'creative' marketing of the self[142] – has dulled the inclination to co-operate. Be that as it may, I suspect (although I could not prove) that most scholars, although both ambitious and rightly proud of their work, would aspire to a more generous mode of academic relationship, if the conditions allowed it. The edited collection at its best offers a model of that community.

One's life in any community involves the acceptance of some mutual obligation, and a realisation that the interests of the whole are sometimes best served by the constraint of one's own. As a contributor, I may have to accept some shaping of my work as I collaborate with an editor to turn my contribution into something that is in dialogue with the other chapters, and helps the whole collection amount to more than the sum of its parts. This may sometimes be an agreeable intrusion, and one that in fact improves my

[141] K. Fitzpatrick, *Generous Thinking: A radical Approach to Saving the University* (Johns Hopkins University Press, 2019), pp. 29–33.

[142] On university staff as part of the 'super-creative core' of a casualised and precarious workforce, see O. Mould, *Against Creativity* (Verso, 2018), pp. 33–6.

work in ways in which I did not expect; at other times it may be less welcome, but still necessary. Although perhaps not all would accept it, I would argue that as a contributor I have also an obligation to the other contributors to the book to commit the time and energy required to produce work of the required standard at the times laid down, or to withdraw in good time if I cannot so commit.

At the same time, these obligations are mutual, or ought to be, but without some level of trust between those involved, such a system is bound to fail. As I recognise my obligation to the other contributors, I am required to take a risk: to trust the other contributors similarly to commit themselves. Just as the editor(s) accept some risk to their reputations in trusting me to contribute, so I must trust the editor(s) to complete their work in a similar fashion. I trust them also to intervene to create the most coherent and impactful work that there can be, even if it involves rejecting the work of others.

And it is here that the misalignment of academic and institutional interests is most obvious. For a university with one eye on its finances and the other on the capriciousness of government policy, to seek to minimise any perceived risk when dealing with centrally administered research assessment is a rational response. Scholars, competing to secure an academic job, or promotion, or tenure, may also be forgiven for trimming their sails to the wind: for aligning their published work with what are thought to be the criteria on which it will be judged. Again, the attempt to mitigate risk is entirely rational. The prevalence of the edited collection meme complex is surely due in part to this risk-averseness. Even if individual works are ostensibly assessed on their own merits, and scholars continue to regard these works as among their best, an ill-defined perception of risk attaches to the format as a whole. The irony is that to dispel that perception, scholars and editors will need to embrace that risk and commit, together, to making the unsuccessful edited collection a thing of the past.

Appendix: Edited Collections Referred to in the Text

Single Volumes

Aylmer, G., and R. Cant, eds (1977). *A History of York Minster*. Oxford: Clarendon Press.

Brügger, N., ed. (2010). *Web History*. New York: Peter Lang.

Brügger, N., ed. (2017), *Web 25: Histories from the First 25 Years of the World Wide Web*. New York: Peter Lang.

Brügger, N. (2018), *The Archived Web*. Cambridge, MA: MIT Press.

Brügger, N., and D. Laursen, eds (2019). *The Historical Web and Digital Humanities: The Case of National Web Domains*. London: Routledge.

Brügger, N., and I. Milligan, eds (2019). *The SAGE Handbook of Web History*. London: SAGE.

Brügger, N., and R. Schroeder, eds (2017). *The Web as History*. London: University College London Press.

Burns, M., and N. Brügger, eds (2012). *Histories of Public Service Broadcasters on the Web*. New York: Peter Lang.

Chapman, M., S. Clarke and M. Percy, eds (2015). *The Oxford Handbook of Anglican Studies*. Oxford: Oxford University Press.

Chapman, M., J. Maltby and W. Whyte, eds (2011). *The Established Church: Past, Present and Future*. London/New York: Mowbray.

Collinson, P., N. Ramsay and M. Sparks, eds (1995). *A History of Canterbury Cathedral*. Oxford: Oxford University Press.

Cooke, M., ed. (1999). *The Cambridge Companion to Benjamin Britten*. Cambridge: Cambridge University Press.

Cross, C., D. Loades and J. Scarisbrick, eds (1983). *Law and Government under the Tudors*. Cambridge: Cambridge University Press.

Dearmer, P., ed. (1933). *Christianity and the Crisis*. London: Victor Gollancz.

Duncan, R., ed. (1948). *The Rape of Lucretia: A Symposium*. London: Bodley Head.

Eliot, S., ed. (2013–17). *The History of Oxford University Press*. Oxford: Oxford University Press.

Gore, C., ed. (1895). *Lux Mundi: A Series of Studies in the Religion of the Incarnation*, 14th edn. London: John Murray.

Goulder, M., ed. (1979). *Incarnation and Myth: The Debate Continued*. London: SCM Press.

Green, M., ed. (1977). *The Truth of God Incarnate*. London: Inter-Varsity Press.

Harvey, A. E., ed. (1981). *God Incarnate: Story and Belief*. London: Society for Promoting Christian Knowledge.

Hick, J., ed. (1977). *The Myth of God Incarnate*. London: SCM Press.

Hobbs, M., ed. (1994). *Chichester Cathedral: An Historical Survey*. Chichester: Phillimore.

Holst, I., ed. (1959). *Henry Purcell, 1659–1695: Essays on His Music*. Oxford: Oxford University Press.

Kennedy, K., ed. (2018). *Literary Britten: Words and Music in Benjamin Britten's Vocal Works*. Martlesham: Boydell and Brewer.

Masanès, J., ed. (2006). *Web Archiving*. New York: Springer.

Mitchell, D., and H. Keller, eds (1952). *Benjamin Britten: A Commentary on His Works from a Group of Specialists*. London: Rockliff.

Morgan, R., ed. (1989). *The Religion of the Incarnation: Anglican Essays in Commemoration of Lux Mundi*. Bristol: Bristol Classical Press.

Moyser, G., ed. (1985). *Church and Politics Today: The Role of the Church of England in Contemporary Politics*. London: T. & T. Clark.

Palmer, C., ed. (1984). *The Britten Companion*. London: Faber.

Platten, S., G. James and A. Chandler, eds (1997). *New Soundings: Essays on Developing Tradition*. London: Darton, Longman and Todd.

Seldon, A., ed. (2001). *The Blair Effect: The Blair Government, 1997–2001.* London: Little, Brown.

Sentamu, J., ed. (2015). *On Rock or Sand? Firm Foundations for Britain's Future.* London: Society for Promoting Christian Knowledge.

Sykes, S., and J. Booty, eds (1988). *The Study of Anglicanism.* London: Society for Promoting Christian Knowledge.

Sykes, S. W., and J. P. Clayton, eds (1972). *Christ, Faith and History: Cambridge Studies in Christology.* Cambridge: Cambridge University Press.

Temple, W. (1941). *Malvern 1941: The Life of the Church and the Order of Society: Being the Proceedings of the Archbishop of York's Conference.* London: Longmans, Green and Co.

Vidler, A., ed. (1962). *Soundings: Essays Concerning Christian Understanding.* Cambridge: Cambridge University Press.

Wainwright, G., ed. (1989). *Keeping the Faith: Essays to Mark the Centenary of Lux Mundi.* London: Society for Promoting Christian Knowledge.

Walker, L., ed. (2009). *Benjamin Britten: New Perspectives on His Life and Work.* Woodbridge: Boydell and Brewer.

Wiegold, P., and G. Kenyon, eds (2015). *Beyond Britten: The Composer and the Community.* Martlesham: Boydell and Brewer.

Cambridge and Oxford 'Histories'

The Cambridge Ancient History. Cambridge: Cambridge University Press (1924–39).

The Cambridge Economic History of Europe. Cambridge: Cambridge University Press (1941–89).

The Cambridge History of the British Empire. Cambridge: Cambridge University Press (1929–59).

The Cambridge History of British Foreign Policy, 1783–1919. Cambridge: Cambridge University Press (1922–3).

The Cambridge History of English Literature. Cambridge: Cambridge University Press (1907–16).

The Cambridge History of India. Cambridge: Cambridge University Press (1922–64).

The Cambridge Illustrated History of Ancient Greece. Cambridge: Cambridge University Press (1998).

The Cambridge Medieval History. Cambridge: Cambridge University Press (1911–1936).

The Cambridge Modern History. Cambridge: Cambridge University Press (1902–12).

The Oxford History of Anglicanism. Oxford: Oxford University Press (2017–18).

The Oxford History of the British Empire. Oxford: Oxford University Press (1998–9).

The Oxford History of Protestant Dissenting Traditions. Oxford: Oxford University Press (2017–18).

Bibliography

American Academy of Arts and Sciences (2015). 'Trends in the price of academic titles in the humanities and other fields', *Humanities Indicators*, retrieved 16 September 2019 from www.humanitiesindicators.org/con tent/indicatordoc.aspx?i=10965.

Anderson, K. (2012). 'Bury your writing – why do academic book chapters fail to generate citations?', *The Scholarly Kitchen*, 28 August, retrieved 1 January 2019 from https://scholarlykitchen .sspnet.org/2012/08/28/bury-your-writing-why-do-academic-book-chapters-fail-to-generate-citations/.

Anon (2015). 'Informa pays £20m for Ashgate Publishing', *The Bookseller*, 29 July, retrieved 7 March 2019 from www.thebookseller.com/news/ informa-pays-20m-ashgate-publishing-308308.

Anon (2017). 'Germans edge towards the brink in dispute with Elsevier', *Times Higher Education*, 7 December.

Anon (2018). 'French say "no deal" to Springer as journal fight spreads', *Times Higher Education*, 12 April.

Anon (2018). 'Plan S "could prove fatal" for learned societies', *Times Higher Education*, 25 October.

Anon (2018). 'Plan S: shock or solution?', *Times Higher Education*, 13 September, p. 15.

Arnold, D. N., and Kristine K. Fowler (2011). Nefarious numbers. *Notices of the American Mathematical Society*, 58(3), 434–7.

Bentley, M. (2005) *Modernizing England's Past: English Historiography in the Age of Modernism, 1870–1970*. Cambridge: Cambridge University Press.

Berlin, I. (1969) *Four Essays on Liberty*. Oxford: Oxford University Press.

Berlin, I. (1994). The Hedgehog and the Fox. In H. Hardy and A. Kelly eds, *Russian Thinkers*. London: Penguin.

Bishop, D. (2012). 'How to bury your academic writing', *BishopBlog*, 26 August, retrieved 1 February 2019 from http://deevybee.blogspot.com /2012/08/how-to-bury-your-academic-writing.html.

Brennan, E. (2016). 'Framing and proposing an edited volume for publication', *Manchester University Press*, 17 February, retrieved 25 March 2019 from www.manchesteruniversitypress.co.uk/articles/framing-and-proposing-an-edited-volume-for-publication/.

British Academy (2016). 'British Academy responds to Lord Stern's independent review of the Research Excellence Framework (REF)', *The British Academy*, 4 April, retrieved 17 December 2019 from www.thebritishacademy.ac.uk/news/british-academy-responds-lord-sterns-independent-review-research-excellence-framework-ref.

British Academy (2019). *Open Access and Book Chapters*. London: British Academy.

von Bülow, C. (2013). Mem. In J. Mittelstraß, ed., *Enzyklopädie Philosophie und Wissenschaftstheorie*, 2nd edn, volume 5. Berlin: Springer, pp. 318–24.

Carpenter, H. (1992). *Benjamin Britten: A Biography*. London: Faber.

Carrigan, M. (2013). 'Some reflections on editing books and special issues while doing a PhD', *Mark Carrigan*, 17 June, retrieved 20 March 2019 from https://markcarrigan.net/2013/06/17/some-reflections-on-editing-books-and-collections-while-doing-a-phd/.

Carter Wood, J. (2018). 'Collections in crisis?', *Obscene Desserts*, 25 February, retrieved 24 April 2019 from http://obscenedesserts.eu/?p=36.

Chadwick, O. (1970). *The Victorian Church: Part Two: 1860–1901*. London: A. & C. Black.

Chapnick, A., and C. Kukuchka (2016). 'The pros and cons of editing a collection of essays', *University Affairs*, 10 May, retrieved 1 March 2016 from www.universityaffairs.ca/career-advice/the-scholarly-edition/the-pros-and-cons-of-editing-a-collection-of-essays/.

Chapnick, A., and C. Kukuchka (2016). 'Choosing the right contributors', *University Affairs*, 13 July, retrieved 22 April 2019 from www.universityaffairs.ca/career-advice/the-scholarly-edition/choosing-right-contributors/.

Clague, T. (2015). 'Unbundling is over-rated: on the value of contributing to an edited book', *LSE Impact Blog*, 5 March, retrieved 1 February 2019 from http://blogs.lse.ac.uk/impactofsocialsciences/2015/03/05/unbundling-is-over-rated-value-edited-books/.

Clark, G. N. (1945). The origin of the Cambridge Modern History. *Cambridge Historical Journal* 8(2), 57–64.

cOAlition S (2019). '10 Principles', *Plan S*, retrieved 1 April 2019 from www.coalition-s.org/principles-and-implementation/.

Collini, S. (1999). Against Prodspeak: 'Research' in the Humanities. In S. Collini, ed., *English Pasts: Essays in History and Culture*. Oxford: Oxford University Press, pp. 233–51.

Collini, S. (2006). *Absent Minds: Intellectuals in Britain*. Oxford: Oxford University Press.

Collini, S. (2017). What's Happening to Universities? Historical and Comparative Perspectives. In S. Collini, ed., *Speaking of Universities*. London: Verso, pp. 15–35.

Crossick, G. (2015). *Monographs and Open Access: A Report to HEFCE*. London: Higher Education Funding Council for England.

Deegan, M. (2017). *Academic Book of the Future Project Report*. London: The Academic Book of the Future, retrieved 10 February 2019 from https://academicbookfuture.org/end-of-project-reports-2/.

Edwards, L. (2012). Editing academic books in the humanities and social sciences: maximising impact for effort. *Journal of Scholarly Publishing* 44 (1), 61–74.

Erb, B. (2013). Beyond WorldCat: accessing scholarly output in books and edited monographs. *The Charleston Advisor*, 15(2), 62–6.

Evans, R. J. (1997). *In Defence of History*. London: Granta.

Farrell, G. (2018). For fairness, we need anonymous marking in the REF, too. *Times Higher Education*, 11 January.

Fischer, K. S., M. Wright, K. Clatanoff, H. Barton and E. Shreeves (2012). Give 'em what they want: a one-year study of unmediated patron-driven acquisition of e-books. *College and Research Libraries* 73(5), 469–92.

Fitzpatrick, K. (2019). *Generous Thinking: A Radical Approach to Saving the University*. Baltimore: Johns Hopkins University Press.

Goldie, M. (2008). Fifty years of the *Historical Journal*. *Historical Journal*, 51 (4), 821–55.

Green, M. (2001). *Adventure of Faith: Reflections on Fifty Years of Christian Service*. Grand Rapids, MI: Zondervan.

Guerin, C. (2014). 'Journal article or book chapter?', *Doctoral Writing Special Interest Group*, 1 May, retrieved 1 August 2018 from https://doctoralwrit ing.wordpress.com/2014/05/01/journal-article-or-book-chapter/.

Hacker, A. (2013). 'In defense of the edited book', *A Hacker's View*, 3 December, retrieved 1 March 2019 from www.andreahacker.com/in-defense-of-the-edited-book/.

Harnad, S. (1986). On reviewing (and publishing in) edited interdisciplinary volumes. *Contemporary Psychology*, 31(5), 390.

Hinchliff, P. (1998). *Frederick Temple, Archbishop of Canterbury: A Life*. Oxford: Clarendon Press.

Horowitz, I. L. (2017). *Communicating Ideas: The Politics of Scholarly Publishing*, 2nd edn. London: Routledge.

Institute of Historical Research (2008). 'Teachers of history numbers', *Making History: The Changing Face of the Profession in Britain*, retrieved 3 April 2019 from www.history.ac.uk/makinghistory/resources/statis tics/teachers.html.

Jordanova, L. (2000). *History in Practice*. London: Arnold.

Jubb, M. (2017). *Academic Books and Their Future: A Report to the AHRC and the British Library*. London: The Academic Book of the Future.

Kelsky, K. (2012). 'Should I do an edited collection?', *The Professor Is In*, 24 July, retrieved 1 June 2018 from http://theprofessorisin.com/2012/07/24/should-i-do-an-edited-collection/.

Keown, D., and C. Prebish (2013). Celebrating twenty years of the *Journal of Buddhist Ethics. Journal of Buddhist Ethics*, 20, 37–9, http://blogs.dickinson.edu/buddhistethics.

Kenyon, J. (1993). *The History Men*, 2nd edn. London: Weidenfeld and Nicolson.

Kerman, J. (1985). *Musicology*. London: Fontana.

Kremakova, M. (2016). 'What's so bad about book chapters? Nothing really', *The Sociological Imagination*, 9 June, retrieved 17 December 2019 from https://web.archive.org/web/20170626034643/http://sociologicalimagination.org/archives/18684.

Larsen, P. O., and M. von Ins (2010). The rate of growth in scientific publication and the decline in coverage provided by Science Citation Index. *Scientometrics*, 84(3), 575–603.

Le Goues, C., Y. Brun, S. Apel et al. (2018). Effectiveness of anonymization in double-blind review. *Communications of the ACM*, 61(6), 30–3.

Linehan, P. A. (1982). The making of the Cambridge Medieval History. *Speculum*, 57(3), 463–94.

Louis, W. R. (1998). Preface. In P. J. Marshall, ed., *The Oxford History of the British Empire. Volume II: The Eighteenth Century*. Oxford: Oxford University Press, pp. vii–ix.

McKitterick, D. (2004). *A History of Cambridge University Press: Vol. 3: New Worlds for Learning, 1873–1972.* Cambridge: Cambridge University Press.

Mould, O. (2018). *Against Creativity*. London: Verso.

Moxham, N., and A. Fyfe (2018). The Royal Society and the prehistory of peer review, 1665–1965. *Historical Journal*, 61(4), 863–89.

Muller, J. Z. (2018). *The Tyranny of Metrics*. Princeton, NJ: Princeton University Press.

Nederman, C. J. (2005). Herding cats: the view from the volume and series editor. *Journal of Scholarly Publishing*, 36(4), 221–8.

OAPEN Project (2014). 'Researcher survey, 2014: report', *OapenUK*, retrieved 30 September 2019 from https://web.archive.org/web/20161012055051/http://oapen-uk.jiscebooks.org/research-findings/researcher-survey-2014/.

Ossenblok, T., R. Guns and M. Thelwall (2015). Book editors in the social sciences and humanities: an analysis of publication and collaboration patterns of established researchers in Flanders. *Learned Publishing*, 28(4), 261–73.

Palgrave Macmillan (2019). 'Editing an essay collection', *Palgrave Macmillan*, retrieved 25 March 2019 from www.palgrave.com/br/palgrave/book-authors/your-career/mid-career-scholars-hub/editing-an-essay-collection/7487710.

Pedersen, S. D. (2011). Festschriftiness. *London Review of Books*, 33(19), 31–2.

Pohl, A. (2014). 'Sammelband herausgeben: gelernt', *Übertext*, 3 June, retrieved 22 April 2019 from www.uebertext.org/2014/03/.

Pontille, D., and D. Torny (2014). The blind shall see! The question of anonymity in journal peer review. *Ada: A Journal of Gender, New Media and Technology*, 4, retrieved 26 March 2019 from https://adanewmedia.org/2014/04/issue4-pontilletorny/.

Ramsey, M. (1960). *From Gore to Temple: The Development of Anglican Theology between Lux Mundi and the Second World War, 1889–1939*. London: Longmans.

Reeve, A. (2013). 'Making edited collections work', *Rowman & Littlefield*, 22 August, retrieved 17 December 2019 from https://web.archive.org

/web/20160306223845/http://www.rowmaninternational.com/com
ment/making-edited-collections-work-a-publishers-perspective.

Research Assessment Exercise 2008 (2006). *Panel Criteria and Working Methods: Panel N*, retrieved 17 December 2019 from www.rae.ac.uk/pubs/2006/01/.

Research Excellence Framework 2014 (2015). *Overview Report by Main Panel D and Sub-panels 27 to 36*, retrieved 17 December 2019 from www.ref.ac.uk/2014/panels/paneloverviewreports/.

Research Excellence Framework 2021 (2019). *Guidance on Submissions*, retrieved 17 December 2019 from www.ref.ac.uk/publications/guidance-on-submissions-201901/.

Rhodes, P. J. (1999). The Cambridge Ancient History. *Histos*, 3, 18–26.

Rice, C. (2013). 'Three simple distinctions your government should eliminate from its research financing system', *Curt Rice*, 7 November, retrieved 30 January 2019 from http://curt-rice.com/2013/11/07/3-simple-distinctions-your-government-should-eliminate-from-its-research-financing-system/.

Rojas, F. (2011). 'Let's talk about edited collections', *orgtheory.net*, 28 July, retrieved 1 March 2019 from https://orgtheory.wordpress.com/2011/07/28/lets-talk-about-edited-volumes/.

Sayer, D. (2014). *Rank Hypocrisies: The Insult of the REF*. London: SAGE.

Seglen, P. O. (1997). Why the impact factor of journals should not be used for evaluating research. *British Medical Journal*, 314, 498–502.

Smith, M. E. (2007). 'Why are so many edited volumes worthless?', *Publishing Archaeology*, 26 August, retrieved 1 May 2019 from http://publishingarchaeology.blogspot.com/2007/08/why-are-so-many-edited-volumes.html.

Smith, R. (2006). Peer review: a flawed process at the heart of science and journals. *Journal of the Royal Society of Medicine*, 99 (4), 178–82.

Soble, A. G. (2003). Review of 'Fact and Value: Essays on Ethics and Metaphysics for Judith Jarvis Thomson'. *Essays in Philosophy*, 4(1), article 5, at https://commons.pacificu.edu/eip/vol4/iss1/5/.

Swords, D. A., ed. (2011). *Patron-Driven Acquisitions: History and Best Practices*. Berlin: De Gruyter.

Tanner, S. (2016). *An Analysis of the Arts and Humanities Submitted Research Outputs to the REF2014 with a Focus on Academic Books*. London: The Academic Book of the Future.

Thompson, J. B. (2005). *Books in the Digital Age: The Transformation of Academic and Higher Education Publishing in Britain and the United States*. Cambridge: Polity Press.

Thomson, P. (2012). 'Is writing a book chapter a waste of time?', *Patter*, 27 August, retrieved 1 September 2018 from https://patthomson.net/2012/08/27/is-writing-a-book-chapter-a-waste-of-time/.

Thomson, P. (2013), 'Two big hassles in editing and what you can do about them', *Patter*, 9 September, retrieved 22 April 2019 from https://pat thomson.net/2013/12/09/two-big-hassles-in-editing-a-book-and-what-you-can-do-about-them/.

Tulving, E. (2007). Are There 256 Different Kinds of Memory? In J. S. Nairne, ed., *The Foundations of Remembering: Essays in Honor of Henry L. Roedinger, III*. New York: Psychology Press, pp. 39–52.

Tyrrell, I. (2005). *Historians in Public: The Practice of American History, 1890–1970*. Chicago: University of Chicago Press.

Vidler, A. (1977) *Scenes from a Clerical Life: An Autobiography*. London: Collins.

Waddell, B. (2019). 'Historians, PhDs and jobs, 1995–96 to 2017/18', *The Many-Headed Monster*, 7 March, retrieved 3 April 2019 from https://manyheadedmonster.wordpress.com/2019/03/07/historians-phds-and-jobs-1995-96-to-2017-18/.

Webster, P. (2013). 'On the invisibility of edited collections', *Webstory*, 14 January, retrieved 1 October 2019 from https://peterwebster.me/2013/01/14/on-the-invisibility-of-edited-collections/.

Webster, P. (2015). 'New British Library metadata for theology and church history', *Webstory*, 4 June, retrieved 3 April 2019 from https://peterwebster.me/2015/06/04/new-british-library-metadata-for-theology-and-church-history/.

Weiler, J. (2016). 'On my way out – advice to younger scholars III: edited book', *Blog of the European Journal of International Law*, 5 October, retrieved 1 March 2019 from www.ejiltalk.org/on-my-way-out-advice-to-young-scholars-iii-edited-book/.

Wilsdon, J., L. Allen, E. Belfiore et al. (2015). *The Metric Tide: Report of the Independent Review of the Role of Metrics in Research Assessment and Management*. London: Higher Education Funding Council for England.

Zeitlyn, D., and M. Beardmore-Herd (2018). Testing Google Scholar bibliographic data: estimating error rates for Google Scholar citation parsing. *First Monday*, 23(11), https://firstmonday.org/ojs/index.php/fm/article/view/8658/7607.

Acknowledgements

This book has its genesis in a conversation following a session of the Digital History seminar at the Institute of Historical Research (University of London) in 2012, and my thanks are due to those attending it for the stimulus first to think about the issue. I am also most grateful to Jane Winters for (much later) commissioning this book and giving me the occasion to think about the edited collection in greater depth. I have also benefitted from conversations with scholars, librarians and publishers on social media, too many to name individually, and in private communications, which must remain anonymous. Particular thanks are due to those who I interviewed, who gave up their time to talk at length about what must have seemed a rather obscure subject, and to those who responded to a survey questionnaire in 2018.

My thanks are due to my former colleagues Simon Baker and Peter Salt of the Bibliography of British and Irish History (at the Institute of Historical Research) for their assistance in providing data not otherwise publicly available, and in answering my queries about it. Thanks are also due to the Royal Historical Society under whose aegis the data has been collected from the outset, and to the BBIH's publisher, Brepols.

At a late stage I had the benefit of conversations with Harriet Barnes and James Rivington (both of the British Academy) in the course of a research project on Open Access and the edited collection, the report of which appeared shortly before this book was completed. Jane Winters, Martin Eve and Tim Hitchcock all read and made many incisive comments on an early draft. I must also thank the two external readers for Cambridge University Press for their comments, which further improved the text. I also gratefully acknowledge the help of Samantha Rayner and Rebecca Lyons, overseers of the Cambridge Elements in Publishing and Book Culture series, and all at Cambridge University Press.

Cambridge Elements ≡

Publishing and Book Culture

SERIES EDITOR

Samantha Rayner
University College London

Samantha Rayner is a Reader in UCL's Department of
Information Studies. She is also Director of UCL's Centre for
Publishing, co-Director of the Bloomsbury CHAPTER
(Communication History, Authorship, Publishing, Textual
Editing and Reading) and co-editor of the Academic Book of
the Future BOOC (Book as Open Online Content) with UCL
Press.

ASSOCIATE EDITOR

Leah Tether
University of Bristol

Leah Tether is Professor of Medieval Literature and Publishing
at the University of Bristol. With an academic background in
medieval French and English literature and a professional
background in trade publishing, Leah has combined her
expertise and developed an international research profile in
book and publishing history from manuscript to digital.

ABOUT THE SERIES

This series aims to fill the demand for easily accessible, quality texts available for teaching and research in the diverse and dynamic fields of Publishing and Book Culture. Rigorously researched and peer-reviewed Elements will be published under themes, or 'Gatherings'. These Elements should be the first check point for researchers or students working on that area of publishing and book trade history and practice: we hope that, situated so logically at Cambridge University Press, where academic publishing in the UK began, it will develop to create an unrivalled space where these histories and practices can be investigated and preserved.

Cambridge Elements ☰

Publishing and Book Culture
Academic Publishing

Gathering Editor: Jane Winters
Jane Winters is Professor of Digital Humanities at the School
of Advanced Study, University of London. She is co-convenor
of the Royal Historical Society's open-access monographs
series, New Historical Perspectives, and a member of the
International Editorial Board of Internet Histories and the
Academic Advisory Board of the Open Library of Humanities.

Elements in the Gathering

A full series listing is available at: www.cambrige.org/EPBC

Printed in the United States
By Bookmasters